Deconstructing Pierre Bourdieu

Deconstructing Pierre Bourdieu

Against Sociological Terrorism From the Left

Algora Publishing
New York

Algora Publishing, New York

Printed in the United States of America
ISBN: 1-892941-53-8
Editors@algora.com

Library of Congress Cataloging-in-Publication Data 00-011298

Verdés-Leroux, Jeannine.
[Savant et la politique. English]
Deconstructing Pierre Bourdieu: against sociological terrorism from the left / by Jeannine Verdés-Leroux.
p. cm.
ISBN 1-892941-53-8
1. Bourdieu, Pierre. 2. Sociology—Philosophy. 3. Sociology—Methodology. 4. Sociology—France—History. I. Title.
HM479.B68 V4713 2000
301'.01—dc21
00-011298

New York
www.algora.com

By the same author:

AU SERVICE DU PARTI, *le parti communiste, les intellectuels et la culture* (1944-1956), Fayard, 1983.

LE RÉVEIL DES SOMNAMBULES, *le parti communiste, les intellectuels et la culture* (1956-1985), Fayard, 1987.

LA LUNE ET LE CAUDILLO, *le rêve des intellectuels et régime cubain* (1959-1970), Gallimard, 1989.

REFUS ET VIOLENCES, *Politique et littérature à l'extrême-droite, des années 1930 aux retombées de la Libération*, Gallimard, 1996.

Édition, introduction et notes de: Boris Souvarine, A CONTRE-COURANT, *Écrits 1925-1939*, Denoël, 1985.

Édition, avant-propos et notes de Philippe Ariès, LE PRESÉNT QUOTIDIEN, *1955-1966*, Éditions du Seuil, 1997.

Table of Contents

Pierre Bourdieu
Or
A Con-Artist's Sociology

It seems daring, even pretentious — and perhaps useless — to attempt to show how limited are Pierre Bourdieu's contributions to sociology and how great are the errors contained in his lessons on method. Pretentious, because Bourdieu is very richly endowed with all kinds of capital (cultural, social and symbolic): Professor at the College of France, Academic Dean at the School of Advanced Studies in Social Sciences, Director of a scholarly review, editor of collections of essays and articles, author of works that are "taught" in high school economics and social studies classes, textbook author, etc., and no doubt many others that have slipped my mind. And useless, for Bourdieu, locked up in his theory for a third of a century, is still denouncing at the top of his lungs the "formidable resistance" aroused by sociological analysis, or at least *his* sociological analysis — for only his sociology is scientific; he claims that "the logic behind this resistance and the ways in which it is manifested are completely analogous to the resistance encountered by psychoanalytical talk."[1] Therefore, when one writes about his sociology and the way he now uses his status as a (critical) intellectual, one can hardly expect to arouse debate, questions or doubt. The whole situation irresistibly calls to mind Trotsky who, after having received a long and critical letter from Boris Souvarine, responded, "Man overboard. Duly noted. And now, on to today's agenda."[2] For a long time now, Bourdieu has been letting us know: "First of all, from now on, I am my own best critic. And that is enough. Magnificently. . . What I have to do is to organize, without disabling my defense. . ." [It was Céline, of course, who made that position famous[3]]. That is why Bourdieu publishes collections of his conferences and his interviews, illustrating and defending his sociology, without missing any opportunity to demolish "faulty" readings. In the last twenty years, he has transformed himself into a sales rep for Bourdieusian thought: and actually, that is one of the most objectionable of his "activities" in the intellectual field.

For such a long time I had been hoping that some of my colleagues, endowed themselves with considerable "capital" in its various forms, would set pen to paper and undertake this criticism, using guns as big as his; for in the university hallways and the cafeteria, ironic and exasperated comments are often heard, followed by great sighs: what are we going to do with him? By which is meant: "How can we cut him down to size, instead of allowing himself to go on promoting himself so noisily. . .?"

However, no such criticism seems to be forthcoming. Therefore I have decided, at the cost of laborious effort and, I must admit, sullenly (for it is exhausting to slog through his writings)[4], to attempt a critical work on an *œuvre* that has enjoyed worldwide distribution and acclaim. Bourdieu's latest books attracted rave reviews and were granted big print runs. His disciples and acolytes apply and apply his theory, seeking to prove its general validity and perfection. This allegiance and nominalism are not exactly creative; his theory serves the function of "lazy securitization" for which he reproached Marxism twenty years ago.[5]

Of course, in specialized journals you can find criticisms of his method or his fundamental concepts (ah! the *habitus*, "'*habitus*, shmabitus, all we ever hear about is *habitus*', mutter the irreverent students at the ENS*", reported Claude Grignon[6]). Perhaps these criticisms were too respectfully given to make any waves. Of course, there have

*École Normale Superieure, a prestigious college in Paris for teachers and academic researchers.

been a few harder hitting attacks — I am thinking, for example, of Michel Deguy's critique of *La Distinction*[7] — but they are partial criticisms. It is not just this or that book by Bourdieu that calls for a vigorous criticism, but his intellectual methods and his overall theory that must be criticized, for his theory rests on a fantasy view of the world. With this worldview as the foundation, Pierre Bourdieu has devoted himself to erecting the framework of a theory, and he has locked himself up in it. There is no use in his repeating, these days, that he never shied away from the "humblest tasks" (!) of the trade[8]; his writings show that he is completely out of touch with the "ordinary" world. The "intentions and principles of the procedures" that he hammers home to us at the end of *The Weight of the World*, for example, only make manifestly clear how unrealistic are his methods — which one doubts were ever applied to the letter — and how many errors he makes in practice (Chapter II).

In one of his many defenses of the scientific nature of his sociological work, Bourdieu spoke about the logic of competition, which is that of all scientific universes, and which "brings to bear on every sociologist the same constraints and controls that it brings to bear, in turn, on all the others"[9]: but how can the "field" of sociology (and the social sciences in general) be constituted — what are the controls that have weighed and continue to weigh upon it? When I consider that Bourdieu is being taught in high schools and colleges, I am tempted to think of his sociological theory in the same terms that he himself wrote about the Marxist vulgate: it has "clouded and confounded the brains of more than one generation".[10]

Pierre Bourdieu's Fantasy World

My goal is to have people take a look (or a fresh look) at the most peremptory and least "scientific" statements of his sociology. Using certain specific texts as examples, I want to show that this sociology, which calls itself scientific — and which the author endlessly praises for its hard-won clarity and the outrageous efforts and vigilance that have gone into it — is based on a catastrophic vision of the social world, of social relations.

The social world that Bourdieu claims to reveal is a projection of his own vulnerabilities, the "wrenchings" that he has suffered, his own "miseries" and his illusions. Sometimes, his particular position in social relations is presented as an asset, one of the conditions of a properly scientific practice: he says he has "a less abstract idea than other people have, of what it is to be a peasant from the mountains", he even claims to have "*by the same token*, a greater awareness of the insurmountable, ineffaceable distance" and to know that familiarity "can be, in principle, both a more acute awareness of the distance and a real proximity".[11] But more often, he refers to his background as a hardship, something that has structured his vision of the world. "I spent most of my youth isolated in a remote village in the southwest of France. And I could satisfy the demands of schooling only by letting go of many of my experiences and much of what I had learned, and not only a certain [regional] accent. . . "[12] He has also said, "In France, the fact that one comes from a remote province, especially one that is located south of the Loire, confers a certain number of characteristics that resemble in some respects the colonial situation. . . . There are subtle and less subtle forms of social racism that cannot fail to engender a certain form of lucidity; the fact of constantly being reminded of one's outsider status encourages a person to perceive things that others cannot see or feel. That being said, it is true that I am a product of the ENS who has betrayed the ENS."[13]

We can leave aside that last bit, as it will come up again later; for he is really the standard product of the ENS prep school and the ENS itself. "Social racism", he calls it; in response to his bellyaching over all that he has had to "put up with", I can only bring to mind one of novelist David Shahar's powerful ideas: "No being exists whose heart was not severely wounded in childhood, enough to serve as a basis for execrable behavior. Everyone bears such scars; the only difference is in how we do it."[14]

> I was shocked by reading his *Inaugural Lesson* at the College of France (1982) [his work has no antecedents; he shows no evidence of intellectual exchange; he says nothing concrete about the lessons to come; and he offers a great deal of tedious and esoteric gibberish]. In order to verify whether my reactions had any bases, I set out to read some thirty Inaugural Lessons given between 1949 and 1982. I chose mostly well-known names and, especially, I sought the most varied disciplines. Through good luck I happened to read the lesson presented by Jacques Prentki, in 1965, inaugurating the chair of Theoretical Physics of Elementary Particles. Before explaining how important the theory of elementary particles is to the comprehension and the interpretation of phenomena — the fundamental aspect of problems — and thus the role this theory plays in the system of knowledge — Jacques Prentki began by acknowledging his indebtedness to his closest collaborators, instructors and colleagues. Originally from Poland, he had experienced "the wave of Nazi cruelty" in his country. He evoked in simple terms the Polish intellectuals who had contributed "to sparing from destruction the priceless treasures of a people which are its culture and its science, by transmitting them to the younger generation. . . . I had the good fortune of being young at that time. . . . We received a very high quality education. During the war, we were even able to conduct practical experiments in physics, which, given Poland's material distress in those years, was quite an exploit".[15] Indeed, "everyone bears his own scars, the only difference is in how we do it".

Pierre Bourdieu, born in a village in the Pyrénées-Atlantiques, son of a civil servant, makes it clear that he had a pathetic childhood. He makes a big deal of the "miseries" he suffered at school (perpetrated by the school), he details his experience at boarding school and how that all influenced the choices he made and his approach to sociology. . . The (little) wounds from his childhood (everything that he had to give up; his accent, the customs he had learned, etc.) led him to describe a hard world, full of resentments, with relations of (symbolic) violence at every turn between the abominable dominant (and, generally, in his writings, the pretentious and ridiculous) figures and those who are dominated — crushed, humiliated, ashamed (see "being ashamed of oneself" in *Distinction*), who are defined by dispossession. This is a personal view of the world; this is not the result of research. Humiliation is not an integral component of a "dominated" position. If the world were really nothing but that, it would be exhausting, intolerable, it would deserve to be destroyed.

To Bourdieu's dark view of the world, I contrast the world of men, the only objects of history, as described by Lucien Febvre: "Men endowed with multiple functions, engaged in diverse activities, of varied aptitudes and concerns, which all mix, conflict, combine themselves and end up concluding between them a peace through compromise, a *modus vivendi* which is called Life".[16]

The world of Pierre Bourdieu is a world of inexorable battles, unforgivable, permanent, eternal, without any respite or escape. Of course, he would protest, there is a way out: see his sociology. He proclaims the liberating functions of a scientific sociology that unveils the relations of domination and provides "the tools for reappropriating the schema of perception and appreciation" that are at the root of a misery that is properly social[17]; and for more than twenty years, he has been overseeing "the dissemination of defensive weapons against symbolic domination"[18]. [Scientific sociology is a political weapon, for the dominated classes: then, is this a proletarian science?] How can he make such a claim, when his writing, which he has voluntarily made complex, even illegible, cannot be read (much less digested!) by any but those who already have in hand all the means of appropriation, etc.?

What about the dominated and the excluded? Bourdieu must have a presentiment that his sociology is of no use to them and does not serve them.

An Artificial Language

One of the first things that strike a reader of Pierre Bourdieu is his writing style (see Chapter I). Always ponderous, and off-putting, he takes the haughtiness of an ENS graduate and adds a pinch of prep-school irreverence (speaking, for example, about "the piss-copy" of the Episcopate, or "la thèse et la foutaise" [roughly translated, "theses and feces").[19]

To justify his laboriously crafted (over-worked) writing, Bourdieu advances various arguments according to the needs of the moment. For example, this mannerism is necessary in order to make an adequate construct of the object; or it is required to reflect the complexity of the object of which he is rendering account; or it is to prevent misreadings.

He constantly justifies the need to resort to an artificial language. "The sociologist must resort to made-up words — words that are, at least relatively, protected against naive projections of common meanings. The more the 'linguistic nature' of these words predisposes them to resist over-hasty readings, the better they are protected against distortion (such is the case with *habitus*, which evokes an asset, or even property, or capital) and perhaps especially when they are inserted, enclosed, in a network of relations imposing their own logical constraints: *allodoxia*, for example — which means something difficult to say or to even to conceptualize in few words — . . . is enmeshed in the network of words with the same root: doxa, doxophobe, orthodoxy, heterodoxy, paradox."[20]

Such an exercise of lofty rhetoric, very frequent in Bourdieu, is not only an exercise in "stylistic arrogance" underscoring the theoretical magisteriality exerted by he who writes; a stereotype of symbolic violence, it functions effectively to protect the statement from any discussion. To speak like Bourdieu — attacking Heidegger — "an ideological production is all the more successful when it can make wrong whoever tries to reduce it to its objective truth".[21]

Thus, Bourdieu inflicts more and more cruel or exotic words on us because he has to do so. It is essential. *Paizein, spoudazein, spoudaiôs paizein, per-spicere, lusiones, eidos, phronesis, toto cœlo, Weltbild, Vorgriffe, Allgemeingültigkeit,* etc.. I was astonished to see, at the end of *Pascalian Meditations*, an *index rerum* and an *index nominum.* Were these words essential to prevent any "distortion"? I must say that the terms *indices rerum, indices nominum,* increased my (already considerable) suspicions in respect to whether Bourdieu's writings could be taken seriously.

In *Free Exchange,* he reflects on esotericism. "I think that one way to solve the problem of being cut off from the public would be to produce messages on several levels. . . That is more or less what we try to do in our magazine *Actes,* by trying to give an analysis (of haute couture, for example) in two ways: through photographs (organized according to a certain structure) and through the analytical text." And he takes on, as usual, the intellectuals who have ended up "admitting that the rift between research and the general public was inevitable" and who are not prepared — whereas he is — to produce messages "on several levels".[22]

When we consider that Bourdieu's scientific sociology aims to provide the dominated — don't forget that — with "the means of dominating domination",[23] this is flabbergasting: both what he proposes (here, an analysis of haute couture) and the fact that he thinks that the dominated classes should be satisfied with (or should make do with) photographs, albeit "organized according to a certain structure". In the end, the analysis is quite short and. . . esoteric. Since he has begun to speak in terms of effectiveness[24], now, he can be answered without hesitation: he is not effective, and to talk about furnishing "weapons" to the dominated in this way is an imposture. Perhaps he realizes this, to some extent, for once he has ensured that his work will get adequate publicity, he speaks with good humor about outspokenness.

Twenty years ago, before an audience of linguists, he defined outspokenness. "One can, as they say, be *outspoken*, one can speak frankly, one can speak freely. This outspokenness is the popular speech in popular situations, when the laws of the market are set aside. But it would be wrong to say that the real popular speech is outspokenness. It is no more real than the other. The truth of popular competence is *also* the fact that, when confronted with an official setting, it breaks down; while on its own ground, in family relations, familiar relations, among its own kind, outspokenness is the rule."[25] Now, Bourdieu says it bluntly: outspokenness should "be the rule in intellectual exchanges",[26] which leads to his so amusing dialogue with his buddy Pécuchet-Haacke in *Free Exchange* (see Chapter VIII).

Outspokenness rang a bell, for me: the professional "reading" that I had done these last years of Céline's works made me familiar with Céline's "frank speech" and his "I understand myself". The author of a recent lampoon against Céline puts it nicely: "Such is the tautology of frank talking: a kind of approval of oneself by oneself, in which one takes one's own side."[27] It would be hard to phrase it better.

Bourdieu's noisy championing of himself makes me laugh, at first — and then it worries me, for it implies a curious understanding of what scholarly communication should be. . . Bourdieu, who warns intellectuals against the "risks of all kinds" that go with "the show" [or the *epideixis* (!), "as the pre-Socratics said"[28](!)], devotes most of his time to his self-commentary and self-promotion: like Céline, and with same verbal inflation, he talks about his loneliness and his lucidity, and the ostracism, the incomprehension from which he suffers. "I have indeed the feeling that I am rather misunderstood."[29] In soliloquies that are a combination of whining and invective, Céline took on the passive resisters of his time; Bourdieu takes on his "Pharisaic" readers, a word that absolutely floors me. Bourdieu, like Céline, wants only devotion, allegiance; they are (both) the only valid critics of their works, of which they are "the master and owner".[30]

The "constructed dialogue" with Loïc J. D. Wacquant illustrates what Pierre Bourdieu calls a dialogue (see Chapter VII).

> Reading Loïc J. D. Wacquant's long introduction to Bourdieu's *œuvre*[31], I found confirmation that the obscurity of Bourdieu's language was necessary indeed; under its complications and its superabundance, Bourdieu manages to mask certain weaknesses of his theory. Loïc J. D. Wacquant, lacking his linguistic mastery, exposes the inconsistencies, the vacuum and the bluff that run through the theory. Bourdieu's writing only "works" only when it is torrential. Isolating a thought from the terroristic sentences, even to admire it, amounts to brutally stripping the thought. For example, Wacquant quotes Bourdieu explaining what is reflexivity: reflexivity requires a systematic exploration of "the inconceivable categories of concepts which delimit the conceivable and which predetermine thought". He does him a poor service, there. [This sentence comes from *The Inaugural Lesson*, p. 7.]

The conduct that Bourdieu is striving to make acceptable in the university milieu, i.e. acting as a self-promoter, seems despicable to me. Each one should make his best efforts in research, and submit his results, which will either be understood and accepted (more or less), or rejected, or ignored, or transformed, or expanded upon, etc., but in the full knowledge that we do not own our work, that we cannot claim to be its sales agent and that we cannot make the promotion of that work our principal task. In his self-promotion, Bourdieu declares himself alone against everybody. Not only is this attitude irritating, but there is an astonishing, enormous gulf between the results that one may read, and what he claims to have established and proven. I resist his theory, as I resist his actions as a manipulator in the intellectual field, and his taking "show business" too far.

But there is one more reason that has led me to respond to his writings: the new figure of the intellectual that he has assumed.

Intellectual Cops

For decades, Bourdieu has been fustigating and sermonizing intellectuals; he does not have harsh enough words to say about their irresponsibility, their vanity, their absence of "critical conscience", "technical skill", "ethical conviction"[32], about their tendency to talk about every topic that presents itself, to "let themselves be carried along by the currents of intellectual history", to "fluctuate with the whims of fashion". "There is something pathetic," he said, "in the docility with which the 'free intellectuals' hasten to present their essays on the trendy topics of the moment. . ."[33] I could cite such quotes by the hundred, Bourdieu is so indefatigable in giving lessons and is equally tireless in passing judgment on others. Of course, he contrasts his own good behavior (1980) to them: "I question this world because it questions me, and in a very fundamental way that goes well beyond the simple feeling of social exclusion: I never feel fully justified in being an intellectual, I do not feel 'at home', I feel that I have accounts to settle — with whom? I have no sense — of what seems to me an unjustifiable privilege. This feeling, which I think I recognize among the socially stigmatized (and Kafka, for example), does not incline me toward immediate sympathy to all those. . . who feel perfectly justified in existing as they exist."[34]

In the introduction to his *Pascalian Meditations*, in 1997, Bourdieu repeats: "I never really felt justified in existing as an intellectual."[35] However Bourdieu, the sociologist of today, has adopted a certain behavior; always prompt to judge others, he allows himself to do as they do. In fact, in December 1980, he was one of a handful of intellectuals who launched an appeal to support Coluche's candidature in the presidential election, invoking democracy (!). Explaining (to everyone else) why they should seriously question the reasons that lead them to accept an invitation to talk on television ["does what I have to say affect everybody? Am I prepared to make my speech, in its form, accessible to everyone? Does it deserve to be heard by everyone? We can even go further: should it be heard by everyone?"[36]], Pierre Bourdieu forgets, in his two lessons on television, to state the reasons (no doubt very carefully pondered) that led him to make up a duet with Abbé Pierre, on public TV.

The Engaged Intellectual

Once upon a time, Bourdieu made fun of intellectuals' public "interventions", of their "mystical participation in the practical". How does he explain his harangue to the railwaymen (December 1995)[37], his systematic signing of every trendy petition, the fact that he allows himself to be caught up by the fads of the moment, the fact that he sees himself as the subaltern (!) and the adviser of unemployed who are up in arms (January 1998), etc.?

This conduct, which he had tirelessly condemned, became good and necessary when it was he who adopted it. Here he is, demanding that the scholar and the artist intervene in the battles of the century: "We are called upon to intervene in the world of the men of power, business, and money, all the more so as they intervene more and more (and more and more effectively) in our world."[38] *The Rules of Art* ends with a chapter calling for "a corporatism of the universal". He calls for a "modern incarnation of the critical power of intellectuals — a collective intellectual, that could give voice to a discourse of freedom, knowing no other limits but the constraints and controls that every artist, every writer and every scholar, building on all that his precursors have achieved, apply to themselves and to all the others".[39] Repudiating the old alternative of engagement or disengagement, he ardently wishes for a genuine *Internationale* of intellectuals, committed to defending the autonomy of the universes of cultural production (which he sees as "very severely threatened" today). . . It seems that he was hardly heard, or heeded. In vain he affirms that we should not accept the leadership of an intellectual in such a movement; intellectuals, at least those in France, know that under the trappings of the "collective intellectual" you will find. . . the hand of Pierre Bourdieu.

Thus, in 1980, Bourdieu changed his posture as an intellectual. One may well wonder why. Is it "the shrewd exploitation of a profitable opportunity"? A way of "selling off the inventory. . . "? Here, reader, you will protest vigorously, and rightly, at seeing such commonplace thoughts and such common words used in speaking about a scholar who tells us time and again that "only technical words enable us to talk about, and thus to think about, and to think rigorously about, difficult things".[40] Could he stoop so low?

Ah, well, such ideas, such words, are expressed in *Actes de la recherche*... where one of Bourdieu's disciples explains to us the effect of viewing the Watteau exhibition (October 1984-January 1985). Before the exhibition, she saw Watteau as a "magical, melancholic painter of grace, of the fragility of a moment of happiness, of the vanity of a love that will turn to disappointment (whose painting, thus, had a metaphysical or at least a psychological impact. . . .)" The similarity, not only of the technique but of the subjects, led her "irresistibly" to a very different interpretation. "One should rather see the shrewd exploitation of a . . . profitable. . . opportunity". This artist, "as shrewd as he was gifted", held up to "the good society of his time" a mirror "that was pleasant and fair to look upon"; "one may believe indeed — but this should be verified — that he had no difficulty in selling all of his inventory".[41] *This should be*. . . a very Bourdieusian phrase, you will note. Before offering such self-assured conclusions, the world of Bourdieu should verify what are only assumptions. Another of Bourdieu's acolytes reminds us that such verification is sorely needed, when she proposes a daring program that *should be* followed[42] [but how?].

Pierre Bourdieu tranquilly, supremely publishes whatever he likes; there is no need to verify, to work patiently, discreetly, for real: whatever he publishes is inevitably scholarly. Moreover, do you think that he verifies his own assertions? For example, he says that pure sciences are, "in part, refuges where one withdraws in order to forget the world, universes purified of everything that causes problems, like sexuality or politics".[43] How would you establish, much less prove, such a proposition? It would be very difficult. Then he repeats this assertion at every opportunity, as if repetition would take the place of proof. Fifteen years later, affirming that "For a teenager, the world of mathematics is the world of the pure, of the free, that enables one to step outside of sexuality and the social", he adds: "Some kind of social psychoanalysis should be made, analyzing the choice of pure sciences as a means of allowing one to hold at arm's length the problems of existence, sexuality and everything else that is dependent on the social".[44]

Re-reading Bourdieu and reading articles like the one on the Watteau exhibition, I have learned how to define Bourdieu's sociology: a con-artist's sociology.

The Function of Metascience

If I have digressed at some length on this Watteau episode, it is because such papers have confirmed what had long been my impression. The avalanche of publications about Bourdieu's research in general, all this metasociology (*Sociology in Question, In Other Words: Essays Towards a Reflexive Sociology, An Invitation to Reflexive Sociology, Practical Reason: On the Theory of Action...*), the way they make such a big deal about how the sociologist works, his false familiarity with his students — to whom the professor at the College of France shows "what can happen in the intimacy of the workshop" ["direct and lasting contact between the ones who teach and the ones who learn" ('Do as I do')[45]], made me think that their results were not so remarkable. The inflation of these self-promoting papers and the claim that the "sciences" give the *modus operandi* and the *opus operatum*, shed light on Bourdieu's writings: few results, but very ambitious programs, and a theory that goes its merry way, safe from being subjected to any real tests... There would be no point in producing a book about books that were judged to be of little interest; but both his theory and his methodology call for criticism — both are, to some extent, talked about, but without being put into practice or with only small amounts of practical application, described in an off-hand and unmethodical way... Thus, as I have already said, no sociologist who was used to field work could ever have written "Understanding", more than twenty pages that Bourdieu tacked onto the end of *The Weight of the World* to teach us how to conduct an interview! It is my exasperation with this piece of anthology (which was greeted with loud reprobation and robust criticism) that impelled me to write a response, and a disrespectful one at that.

The writing of this little text, *La Contre-indication* [*Contra-Indications*] (see Chapter II) led me to re-read all of Bourdieu's books. How can so many errors be stated with so much arrogance, so much priggish pedantry? How can so many burlesque proposals be reiterated without anybody retorting?

Bourdieu is fascinated by Duchamp, and his favorite story about him is this: "I take the urinal and, by virtue of putting it in a museum, I change its nature — because the museum will operate upon it the same effect that it exerts upon any object that is exhibited."[46] The production of belief: here is one of Bourdieu's favorite tenets. He "believes" that he can say and impose anything (the equivalent, if one may say so, of Duchamp's urinal), because consecration (by the College, etc.) makes people "believe". Is Bourdieu naive? The College is not absolute consecration nor does it promise the immortality of one's work.

> Pierre Bourdieu should read the merciless correspondence between Lucien Febvre — just promoted to professor at the Collège de France — with Marc Bloch, and then weigh up the portrait they make of some of Febvre's colleagues and thus of his predecessors![47] [As for Duchamp's urinal, isn't that above all an expression of the artist's impotence?] Bourdieu should produce, rather than giving us these endless lectures and "gestures". He has given himself a position as "a hero of science", a kind of twin to the Bolshevik man invented by Lenin and described so well by Harold Rosenberg.[48]

"*The Hero of Science*"

By evoking his childhood and the school that obliged him to relinquish of his earliest experiences, by talking about his entry into "sociology" — obliging him "to tear up the allegiances and the identity by which one makes oneself part of a group", "to abjure the beliefs that are constitutive of belonging" and "to disavow any bond of filiation and affiliation",[49] Bourdieu makes a point of showing us that the sociologist (Bourdieu) never rests in his (painful) efforts, that he strives tirelessly to control, surmount, limit, master, reduce, thwart (the reader should feel free to add to this list all the words that are so routine in Bourdieu's rhetoric of intimidation), the presuppositions, assumptions, effects, distortions, biases, etc. (just fill in the words that you run across at the beginning of every chapter. . .). Science is what happens in the rupture, let us emphasize; and the word "rupture" is kicked around under his pen as if the word caused the fact. The sociologist (Bourdieu), like the Bolshevik invented by Lenin, requires "an effort of self-transformation, an effort that one can never put aside without running the risk of sliding backwards".[50] Bourdieu talks to us so often and so emphatically about his efforts, his "enormous efforts", that I understood why reading his books seems to me so exhausting: he curses these challenges and the scope, the disproportion of his solitary combat, perhaps lost in advance. This tone is tiresome and laughable. "Conscious of all the expectations that I was constrained to oppose, of all the unquestioned dogmas of 'humanistic conviction' and the 'artistic' faith that I was obliged to defy, I have often cursed the fate (or logic) that forced to me to take such a weak position, knowing full well the consequences, to engage with no weapon but rational speech in a combat that may have been lost in advance against disproportionate social forces. . . ."[51]

Bourdieu wants the reader, like himself, to engage all his being. . . I found Bourdieu's lessons strange and risible: why was he always repeating the same thing, did he think we were deaf or retarded? Harold Rosenberg's pages on Lenin gave me a key. It is because, like Lenin, he has the unshakeable conviction that his line is the right line, and on the basis of this conviction he wants to direct, and control, the activities of others.

Of course, he recognizes two kinds of readers: disciples, those who practice and apply his theories (however, there must not be too many of them, or they are not very appreciative, for nowadays he says, as I have mentioned, that he has been rather inadequately understood), and many more, thus, of the other kind of reader, the slow, the backward, "those who reflect on the social sciences without practicing them" and "those who practice them without reflecting" — for aside from him, himself, who knows that problems are inseparably practical and theoretical, that "scientific practice cannot escape the theory of practice",[52] he believes that we all live in empiricism or in the clouds. Therefore he harps on the same lessons over and over, with a mixture of patience and impatience, on his example (he wants to inculcate in us a general disposition to "sociological invention"), on his conclusions and his discoveries, even if some of these conclusions were understood without his theory — so that some of his discoveries are not exactly new — for example, "cultural capital goes to cultural capital". That is a "social law" and he claims to be its father.[53] While his conclusions and his discoveries do not always take the public by storm, that is not because the public is "malevolent" or pusillanimous ["truths that one prefers not to hear"[54]]; it is because Bourdieu, bound up in a system of references that is often very philosophical and not very open to the work of his contemporaries (although in his *Inaugural Lesson* he speaks of "the already immense achievements of the discipline" — without going into any of them[55]], uses fine words to utter clichés with great solemnity, sometimes reminding the reader of Bouvard and Pécuchet, or sometimes of characters from Ionesco, in a land of untruth.

The parallel with Lenin goes a long way, in my eyes, for it renders comprehensible the apparent singularity of Bourdieu. He keeps saying, "I do not like the intellectual in me"[56]. I have come to understand that this is because he wants to be something other than an intellectual; in both Lenin and Bourdieu, the breadth, the disproportion of the ambition is striking, as is the preeminent, crushing role that they assign to themselves. Under the proclaimed ideology, we find the same lack of sympathy for "the people", for the "dominated", in association with a conspicuous demagoguery that celebrates these same "people". Thus Lenin "would go out *incognito*, to buttonhole ordinary people in Moscow, speaking with the man in the street, the workman and the peasant, to find out their real opinion about the Bolshevik cause", but that was so that he could reduce the "real socialists" to silence.[57] Similarly, Bourdieu says that his surveys for *The Weight of the World* "are a service to the most underprivileged people". "When you want somebody who is not a professional of the word to find a way to say something (and often, such a person will then say something completely extraordinary, something that people who have had the opportunity to speak out for too long would never even think of), you have to work to help him speak. . . I would say that that is the Socratic mission in all its splendor."[58]

The interview with Ali and François, on whom Bourdieu constantly imposes words and ideas (see Chapter II), is a curious case of helping someone to put his thoughts into words. In any case, Bourdieu may not fulfill the "Socratic mission" at all, but he has a solid intention: to take the microphone away from "those who have had the opportunity to speak out for too long", for example, the intellectuals whom he targets in *On Television.*

The "Lesson on The Lesson", or the Opposite of a Lesson

The Inaugural Lesson that he gave at the College of France in 1982 would have been a good occasion for "the hero of science" to describe his contributions to his discipline. "The Lesson" has, indeed, its own rites, it meets certain expectations, it fulfills the obligations of "scientificity" and also of civility[59]. Usually, these lessons include an acknowledgement of the people (professors at the College or others; see, for example, Jacques Monod), both French and foreign (see, for example, Jean-Marie Lehn), to whom the newly elect knows he is indebted to some extent, and even to a great extent. Usually, the discipline is summarized (see, for example, François Jacob), especially if it is young and difficult to comprehend (Jacques Prentki says that his subject matter is difficult, for the language of mathematics "is by no means universal"); sometimes the context of the professorship is discussed — how it fits into the context of the teaching of the discipline at the College (for example, André Pézard talks about the course on Italian literature, André Dupont-Sommer evokes Renan, whose vacant chair he fills, after an interruption); some talk about themselves for their choices and their disciplines are related to their personal backgrounds (for example, the Strasburger Robert Minder teaching literatures of Germanic origin). They all mention their recent works and they spend part of the lesson talking about the work they plan to do in the years to come. Some "Lessons" that I will take care not to quote are dazzling in clarity, talent, simplicity; "personalities", characters are compelling. Many — certainly not all — are a very great pleasure to read and they encourage one to reflect on fundamental questions.

Pierre Bourdieu does not thank anybody; he is not indebted to anyone for anything; he does not owe his science, his career, his election to anybody. He says only one word to those — in particular André Miquel — who made a point of welcoming "an under-appreciated and under-paid science" (p. 35). He professes his freedom with respect to the institution of freedom, attached as he is to "defending liberty with regard to institutions — which is a pre-condition of science" (p. 35). [Isn't this lesson on liberty a little out of place? Without even mentioning more recent examples, we should recall that Michelet and Renan, for example, had to pay the price for their freedom of thought. Has Bourdieu examined the "subversive" nature of his thought, cherished as it is by "the apparatuses of celebration"?] He has the freedom to discover that which sociologists are unable to see ["because they need (it) too much]: "the real basis of the exorbitant power that all the important social sanctions exert, all the symbolic ruckus, the awards, decorations, crosses, medals and ribbons, and all the social supports of the vital *illusio*, the missions, functions and vocations, mandates, ministries and magisteries" (p. 34). He acknowledges, at the end of his discourse, that his "reflexive turn" "may seem somewhat strange or insolent. . . " (p. 35).

The Lesson is especially striking because the discipline has no history, practically no fathers nor antecedents. Bourdieu briefly quotes Durkheim, but immediately cites his limitations: "when it came to his social position as a leading thinker, (he) had trouble holding the social at a sufficient distance to consider it as such" (p. 7). He quotes Marx, "initiator" of the sociology of knowledge, and points out that "those who make a profession of Marxism have never really subjected Marx's thought and especially its social applications" to the test of the sociology of knowledge (pp. 7-8). He quotes Raymond Aron: "This iconoclastic science of aging societies can contribute at least to making us to some extent masters and owners of social nature, by promoting the knowledge and the awareness of the mechanisms that are at the bottom of all forms of fetishism. I am thinking, of course, of that which Raymond Aron (who illustrated this teaching so well) calls 'secular religion'" (p. 21).

Given that Bourdieu makes a passing reference to "the already immense achievements of the discipline" (p. 16), it is all the more peculiar not to see him quoting other sociologists. What are these achievements, and where did they come from?

Bourdieu spends most of his time repeating that sociology is a science (he uses the words *science* and *scientist* more than 70 times in one hour) and that it is not well-liked, but rather dreaded, attacked, and wrongly criticized. It is hard to choose which phrases to quote, to single out just a few statements: "the status of Sociology as a science is always under attack, and most of all, of course, by all those who need the shadows of ignorance to ply their trade in symbols" (p. 14). "Obviously, the existence of sociology as a scientific discipline is always under threat. There is a structural vulnerability inherent in the fact that the game of politicization can always cheat with the scientific imperatives; this means that Sociology has to fear the powers that expect too much from it almost as much as those who want to do away with it" (p. 17). "The labor necessary to bring the truth to light and to get it recognized once it has been produced runs up against the collective defense mechanisms that tend to ensure deep-seated denial, within Freud's meaning. Since the refusal to recognize a traumatic reality is always proportionate to the interests defended, we can understand the extreme violence of the reactions and resistance, among those who possess cultural capital, engendered by any analyses that shed light on the denied conditions of production and reproduction of culture" (pp. 19-20). "The adversaries of sociology are right to wonder whether an activity that supposes and produces collective denial should exist; but nothing gives them the right to dispute its scientific character" (p. 20).

Bourdieu reminds us of what scientific criticism must be: "Science is reinforced whenever scientific criticism is reinforced, that is, inseparably, the scientific quality of the weapons available and the need to use the weapons of science and only them, to triumph scientifically" (p. 15). We are to understand that, unfortunately, many instances wherein the criticism of (scientific) sociology have been practiced have "discredited the profession" (!) (p. 16).

Attacking those who possess cultural capital, Bourdieu hints at the essence of his contribution; his object was to scientifically reconsider the scientific world or, more broadly, the intellectual world (p. 14); he formulated the laws of social reproduction (p. 13). "Spelling out a social law, such as that which holds that cultural capital goes to cultural capital, makes it possible to introduce 'modifying elements', as Auguste Comte said, among the circumstances that are liable to contribute to the effect that it describes — in this particular case, eliminating from school those children who are most lacking in cultural capital — elements which, however weak they are in themselves, may be enough to transform (in the desired direction) the result of the mechanisms" (p. 13).

Thus you may understand that Bourdieu's science is liberating; sociology does not have a mission, nor a mandate (p. 18), but it has liberating virtues. In short, the sociologist knows what he is doing (at the College of France): "There is no sociologist who would take the risk of destroying the thin veil of faith (or bad faith) that is the charm of all institutional pieties, if he did not have faith in the possibility, and the need, to make universal the freedom that sociology provides with regard to the institution; if he did not believe in the liberating virtues of what is undoubtedly the least illegitimate of the symbolic powers, that of science, especially when it takes the form of a science of the symbolic powers that can restore to the social subjects control of the false transcendences that are continually created and recreated out of ignorance" (p. 36). Such is the conclusion of the lesson.

Through his "Lesson on the lesson", Bourdieu shows what he thinks is scientific: taking the opposite tack. Now he tells us, with a new word that repaints his old refrains in a new hue, that his sociology is reflexive and "non-narcissistic" (!). But what is most aggravating in this lesson is that Bourdieu speaks only on his own behalf: he has no ties, no colleagues, no sociologists to quote, no one else's works from which he might borrow. He thinks alone; although on another day he assures us: "I do not mean to imply . . . or claim . . . the status of a great initiator, of a 'creator who was not himself created', who owes nothing to anybody."[60] His sociology often repudiates his meta-sociology.

The aridity of his work is certainly due to the writing style but also to the lack of openness to other thoughts, other work. He says that he works like any "scientist" of the exact sciences: however, this reclusive attitude, bottled up in his own thoughts, ignoring exchanges and interplay, in no way resembles (true) scientific practice — even though he affirms that his work "has always been supported by other scientists", without specifying who they are.[61] If that is the case, perhaps one can assume that these scientists have read (a bit of) his metascience, and that they trust his "intentions" and his (indisputable) talents as Bourdieusian sales rep, but that they have not read his research works and his "results". Once, Bourdieu cited Hume, without any further reference: "Victory is so often won not by the men-at-arms, who wield the halberd and the sword, but by the trumpets, the drums and the musicians of the army."[62] Let us admit that he plays the trumpet very well indeed — that of Fame.

The "Opus Operatum"

Bourdieu repeats compulsively that what defines him is his *opus operandi*. We should ask what this *opus operandi* has led to, in short, we must examine his *opus operatum*, pointing out along the way that this opposition takes a somewhat amusing form and especially that the priority given to the *opus operandi* seems by no means a proof of scientific authenticity. His entire sociology seeks to show how the forms of symbolic violence contribute to the reproduction of domination. The essence of his conclusions concerns the sociology of teaching and the sociology of culture. Bourdieu adds to this a sociology of the State, calling these "three instances of the same effort of re-appropriating the social unconscious", a remark that seems calculated more to impress than to explain his thought process.[63]

Bourdieu affirms that, unlike "speculative sociologists", he "blows to bits" the concept of "the State";[64] he describes the State as an ensemble of fields where forces belonging to the public sector (ministries, services, "corps") vie with each other and, just as in the private sector (banks, construction firms, etc), what is at stake in these battles is "the monopoly of legitimate symbolic violence", i.e. "the power to constitute and to impose as *universal* and *universally applicable* within the scope of a nation. . . a common set of coercive standards". In other words, "The concept of the State makes sense only as a kind of *shorthand designation* (but, for that reason, very dangerous) of the *objective relations* between positions of power (of various types) that may fall within more or less stable networks (of alliances, clients, etc.) and that manifest in interactions that are phenomenally very different, ranging from open conflict to more or less hidden collusion."[65]

Talking about the genesis of the modern state,

"simplifying greatly" (he warns), he explains that the construction of the State is the process of concentration of various types of power or capital, leading to the emergence of a governmental form of capital, which makes it possible for the State to exert power over the various fields and the various forms of capital. This meta-capital defines the State power. . . "The construction of the State goes hand in hand with the construction of the field of power, to be understood as the playing field upon which those who have capital. . . fight *especially* for power over the State, i.e. for the State capital that confers power over the various forms of capital and the means of reproducing them (through, in particular, the institution of the school)."[66] That was in 1987-1988; Bourdieu soon changed his tune.

In 1989, he published *The State Nobility*, the focal point of his work on the State, he says, and in 1990, he published his writings on family economics. In 1993, he published an alarm, *The Weight of the World*, and blamed "resignation" within the government. "The truth of what is going on in the 'difficult neighborhoods' [housing projects] is not inherent in these usually forgotten places", he wrote; it is neo-liberalism, which inspired the measures enacted in the 1970's in regard to the public financing of housing, which determined how the various social categories are distributed in geographic space. "It is the abdication of the State and the public funding for construction. . . which is responsible, essentially, for the dismal appearance of the places where these people are concentrated, where, under the effect of the economic crisis and unemployment, the most deprived populations are relegated." [Does this mean that in times past, there was no social division of space, and there was less social segregation?] So he tackles the neo-liberal vision to which the socialist leaders had subscribed — "the new intellectual guides" who collaborated in "the demolition" of the idea of public service ("through a series of forgeries in theoretical writing and faked equations"), and of course "the upper nobility of the State, molded by the ENA [the prestigious graduate school for public administration] and polished by the teachings of Sciences Po [the political science university]", these "new mandarins who are so avid for favors and bonuses, always looking for ways to make a lucrative leap to the private sector, who, tired of preaching the spirit of 'public service', . . . or worshiping the religion of private enterprise, . . . claim to manage the public services like private companies".[67]

Abruptly, Bourdieu decides not only to respect the State, but to like it; its "abdication" makes him fear that it will disappear. What is the State? It is "a singular universe, whose official goal is public service, service to the public and devotion to the general interest". Of course there have also been, he announces, cases of public trading of favors, embezzlement of public funds, etc., but nonetheless it is still "an extraordinary historical invention, an asset to humanity on a par with art or science. A fragile achievement, always threatened with regression or disappearance. And that is what we today are relegating to the past".[68]

A close friend of researchers "who look at things up close" (but constantly warning against "empiricist illusions", who believes that it is sufficient to "go and see"[69]), Bourdieu had gone to take a close look at housing policies. And that is where he witnessed the process of abdication on the part of the State, which began in the 1970's, and he affirmed at the time, "so much the better. By falling into line with the cult of private enterprise and profit, in around 1983-1984, the socialist leaders have orchestrated a sea change in the collective mentality". And, to a journalist from *L'Express* who asked him whether the socialist leaders were thus jeopardizing "the essential functions of the State", he answered: "Exactly."[70] Apparently, his views have changed.

Having mastered the *ars combinatorial*, "which makes it possible to generate endless speeches by 'stringing together problems the way you thread beads'",[71] Pierre Bourdieu has two languages, one sociological, the other one "ordinary". In his seminars, the Professor gives a view of State power that is close to Weber's — the State is a coercive body — even though he reproaches Weber for having preferred the concentration of the capital of physical force whereas he was more interested in the concentration of symbolic capital. In his free time, citizen Bourdieu seems to be a disciple of Jules Ferry, speaking about the State's dedication to the general interest — whereas in his scholarly writings, he holds official representations of the State as the locus of "universality and the service of the general interest" to be a symbolic construction that presents as legitimate, and disinterested, the universalist representation of domination.[72]

I thus leave aside his sociology of the State, and I don't think we'll be missing much for, speaking in *L'Express* of the State as an "asset to humanity", as a unique universe "whose official goal is public service", he repeats "on his own account, a concept of the State", applies to the State "categories of thought produced and guaranteed by the State" (imposed by school, in particular), therefore ignoring "the most fundamental truth of the State". What has become of his intention to apply "a kind of *hyperbolic doubt* to the State and the concept of the State"? Has he, too, been invented by the State that he thought he was inventing?[73]

Bourdieu's books, which constitute the essence of his sociology of teaching, tackle the "republican" myth of the school as liberator, to reveal the true social functions of the institution, "i.e. one of the bases of domination and the legitimization of domination".[74] Although one faithful follower recently spoke, in connection with *The Inheritors* and *Reproduction*, of "cult books that have marked generations of intellectuals",[75] I believe that it would be worthwhile to recall the books' conclusions.

The Inheritors (in collaboration with Jean-Claude Passeron, 1964) can be summarized by the idea that underneath the apparent "natural" inequalities, we must methodically detect the socially conditioned cultural inequality. The authors outlined what it would take to achieve a real democratization of education based on a rational pedagogy, i.e. a pedagogy founded on a sociology of cultural inequalities, but which could not "really come into being unless all the conditions were met for a real democratization of the recruitment of teachers and pupils, starting with the introduction of a rational pedagogy".[76] I must be one of those poor readers, for this proposal seems me to fall into a vicious circle.

Reproduction in Education, Society and Culture (in collaboration with Jean-Claude Passeron, 1970) tries to prove that in today's bourgeois society, the school system serves as a means of legitimizing the social order and as a way of transmitting privileges to the next generation. "The heir to middle-class privileges relies these days on school certification, which attests to his talents and his merits". The "right" schools ensure not only "the discreet succession rights of the bourgeoisie" but at the same time convinces the disadvantaged that they owe "their school history and social destiny to their lack of talent or merits. . ." for when it comes to culture, "absolute dispossession excludes the consciousness of dispossession".[77]

Homo Academicus (1984) takes the university field, or more precisely, how it operates, as its subject. I cannot emphasize enough the very partial, and not sacrilegious, as Bourdieu claims, nature of the description that he gives. The book takes on certain agents, without discussing what they teach or what they produce, and only discusses what they covet, that is, power and profit, since the various forms of power are what underlie one's choices in taking intellectual positions. The book thus describes the battles of a corporation. Bourdieu likes to hold up this work as a model — he calls it difficult and daring, since the sociologist who managed to produce it was caught up in the very world that he objectified. Later, he made much of what he called the profound "subject" of the book: "the reflexive turn which is implied in objectivizing one's own universe, and the radical threat implicit in the 'historization' of an institution that is socially recognized as having been founded to claim objectivity and universality for its own objectification. . ."[78] He speaks about this book very often, and says that what is important is not what it reveals as to the operation of the university, and academe, but the method that it exemplifies, "a kind of sociological test of sociological practice itself". He goes on at length, at every opportunity, on the controlled relationship with the object that he seems to be the only one [or nearly so] to have managed to achieve, for "one of the chief sources of error in the social sciences resides in an uncontrolled relationship with the object, which results in projecting this un-analyzed relation onto the object of the analysis".[79] However, in this book, his relation with the object seems to have been thought through very little; the object that he has decided to analyze is a small piece, arbitrarily carved out of the stated object, the university field; Bourdieu has never explained why he focuses only on this aspect, while pretending to speak about the whole (see Chapter V).

The State Nobility (1989) studies the French equivalent of the Ivy League schools, showing how the nobility of the State apparatus (especially the staff of the principal institutions of the State) was constituted; they enjoy so many forms of power — intellectual, bureaucratic, political, and economic — that they dominate contemporary society. This big book which, in its desire to fit in, speaks of tearing up "the screen of evidence that masks the familiar world from our knowledge". The book says (verbosely, and in minute detail) how the protected universe of preparatory classes — which have a high productivity (more than the university departments!), by imposing a sense of urgent competition, leads to the production of "*forced intelligences*, a little immature, which, more or less as Sartre writes in connection with some of his readings at the age of twenty, understand everything luminously and do not understand anything absolutely".[80] The action of teaching served above all to produce a separate and sacrosanct group.

Bourdieu affirms (or rather reaffirms) that we, "ordinary readers", see the school institution as an educational enterprise that sanctions, by patents of technical qualification, the acquisition of competence in various fields. He admits that school contributes "to disseminating knowledge and skills" but much more, he says, it contributes to the reproduction of social competences; it contributes "even more, to the distribution of powers and privileges and to the legitimization of this distribution".[81] He unfurls his theory both roundly, i.e. without holding back, and lengthily: you read one copious and predictable section covering the leading schools and their transformations, then a copious and predictable section on power and its transformations. You can almost read it with your eyes closed, Bourdieu takes his repetitions so far. Almost at the end of the work, we even come, once again, to the famous "embarrassment" that his scholarly analyses cause by "bringing to light the way the institution of the school contributes to preserving the social order".[82] This fat tome once again claims to be a study of the — new — form of division of the labor of domination.

To help us comprehend how the scientific method should subvert the social hierarchy of objects, Bourdieu needed Parmenides (!) dialoguing with Socrates on objects that are "ridiculous" or "of no value nor importance"... Parmenides said to Socrates, new to philosophy, that "philosophy will captivate him one day and will show him the vanity of that scorn in which logic has no part". All that, to inform us that we must tackle "wretched", "unworthy", "discredited" objects. For Bourdieu (the scientist), there is no division between objects that are futile or serious, interesting or commonplace, noble or vulgar. And that is why he was ready to talk about photography, or about shopping for socks and slacks.

But having taken enormous efforts to reveal to us "fields that are located lower down in the hierarchy of legitimacies",[83] he seems not to have had enough time to present domination in all its complexity, its subtlety. However, in a conference given in the United States (1989), he explains what domination is not and what it is. It "is not the direct and simple effect of actions exerted by an ensemble of agents ('the dominant class') invested with the power of coercion but the indirect effect of a complex ensemble of actions which are generated within the network of constraints that connect each of the dominant agents, who thus are dominated by the structure of the field through which domination is exercised, and who thus undergo domination on the part of all the others".[84] Where are the practical exercises that would allow us to see, to touch, this complex ensemble of actions, etc.?

> Bourdieu always makes a point of underscoring what others have not seen, have not understood, have omitted, and the ways in which he is distinguished, etc.. Thus he makes a point of affirming and pointing out "all the differences" that separate his theory of symbolic violence "from the Foucaldian theory of domination as discipline and training".[85] Elsewhere, he stresses that Elias "always omits to ask who benefits and who suffers from the State monopoly on legitimate violence" and to ask the question "of the domination that is exerted through the State", whereas he asked it in *The State Nobility*[86], etc.. Domination, power, legitimacy are constantly cropping up in his work; his view of domination is complex in commentary and definitions, but it is summary in the practical exercises...

Intrepidly, at the beginning of his career, he had attacked a "middle brow art"— photography — and devoted a whole research series to it (in 1965). That was, without a doubt, "a special opportunity to exercise, with complete freedom, and to attain by proxy, on the basis of the homology that is established between fields of unequal legitimacy, the fetishized social mechanisms which also function under the censures and the masks of authority in the protected universe of high legitimacy".[87] [Whence the great interest which he also evinced with regard to haute couture.[88]] In *A Middle Brow Art*, he spells out his "social definition of photography". His conclusion appear to be unsurprising:

"For the popular and middle classes, the esthetics which is expressed in the practice of photography and in the criticism of photography as well seems to be a dimension of the ethos, so that the aesthetic analysis of the great mass of photographic works legitimately can be reduced, without being reductive, to the sociology of the groups that produce them, of the functions that they assign to them and of the significances that they confer upon them, explicitly and especially implicitly."[89] Later, in this arena too, he would announce the importance that such a study may have: an analysis of the relations between the popular classes and photography makes it possible to tackle the question of realism and formalism in art.[90] This topic is, as so often happens, offered as a kind of suggestion, never fulfilled.

The Love of Art: European Art Museums and Their Public

(1969) was based on a huge survey of the public visiting European museums of art: fourteen museums in four European countries, twenty French museums. It was supplemented by a mail survey involving members of the Society of the Friends of the Louvre and by research into art instruction in colleges in Paris and the provinces, in general education high schools and technical schools.[91] This enormous and expensive research project arrived at a clear conclusion: "Unrestricted entry is also optional entry, reserved for those who, endowed with the faculty to appropriate the works of art, have the privilege of using this freedom and who are thereby legitimated in their privilege, i.e. in the ownership of the means of appropriating the cultural goods. . . "

Bourdieu recognized that, perhaps, certain people might find that he had expended an enormous effort to state something that was already obvious. But he made a point of saying, or of hammering home, rather, that the sanctification of art served "a vital function": it contributes to consecrating the social order. "For the men of culture to believe in barbarity and to persuade their barbarians within their own barbarism, it is necessary and it is sufficient that they manage to dissimulate themselves and dissimulate the social conditions that make possible not only culture as second nature. . . but even more, the legitimated domination (or, if one wants, legitimacy) of a particular definition of culture."

He explained *ad infinitum* that the heir to middle-class privileges relies on culture as second nature, on "class", on education ("in the sense of a product of the education process which seems to have nothing to do with education"), on "distinction" (italicized in the text), "a merit that was not acquired and which justifies acquisitions that are not merited, i.e. heritage".[92]

This work was yet another occasion to repeat all the evils of school: it is the institution that "transforms the socially conditioned inequalities before culture into inequalities of success, interpreted as inequalities of talent which are also inequalities of merit" (p. 164). Let us summarize: the function of culture is thus to legitimate inherited privileges, to separate the barbarians from the civilized. This assertion is belabored in various forms that very closely resemble each other; but one can hardly say that it has been proven.

The questionnaires used (published pp. 174-180) sought to make it possible to verify a coherent system of theoretical propositions elaborated on the basis of previous research on the processes of cultural diffusion. Although he acknowledged that a questionnaire on this topic was not easy to compose or to administer, Bourdieu showed that he already had well in mind that which he wanted to find; he knew that in a field "where the subjects engage values", "they are inspired, even unconsciously, to elevate themselves by tending toward the answer that they consider noblest" (p. 21). It should be noted that Bourdieu, who always claims to follow other people's unconscious, cannot follow his own: the association culture/dominant is so strongly anchored in his unconscious that he has no need to establish it. And that is why, thirty years after *The Love of Art*, Bourdieu (who is now entirely dedicated to the anti-neoliberalism crusade) can affirm, in a university setting and not in a protest meeting or on the street: "Without knowing anything about the president of the Bank of Germany, I am persuaded that in his leisure hours, like Mr. Trichet, the director of our national bank, he reads poetry and practices patronage."[93]

With *Distinction* (1979), Bourdieu announced a project with broad ambitions: to analyze relations between taste and the conditions of existence (social class), to produce a picture (a table) of lifestyles that would lead to a social criticism of judgment. I will not digress here on that book; two chapters (III and IV) discuss it in order to demonstrate and criticize in particular the sociologist's relationship to the material (which, moreover, was extremely heteroclite) on which he says he has built his analysis. In fact, his very abundant comments develop his fantasy view of the world: in this universe of the dominant and the dominated, the popular classes of the 1970's are shown as humiliated people who feel unworthy, ashamed of themselves; people who "confirm — through feelings of incompetence, of failure or of cultural unworthiness — a kind of recognition of the dominant values".[94] Making a virtue out of necessity... And necessity, in the case of the popular classes, is "the inescapable deprivation of necessary goods".[95] His miserable, anachronistic representations are more like the slogans of the late *Cause du peuple* than a "scientific" view; this view pre-existed any groundwork. [We should ask Bourdieu how he would describe the situation of today's unemployed workers, when he already said that the popular classes of the 1970's were deprived of necessary goods.] The sociologist combines a scornful and envious view of the dominant with a scornful and irritated view of the "dominated", such as he has fabricated them. On what basis does Bourdieu talk about feelings of "shame" that the dominated classes are supposed to feel?

In 1992, Bourdieu published *The Rules of Art*, which proclaimed an ambitious plan: to found a science of cultural production. As he himself has said, hundreds of times, "What is most important is not so much the results themselves as the process by which they are obtained."[96] Or, if you prefer, the *modus operandi* is more important than the *opus operatum*. The results, here, are extremely difficult to grasp; and so is the process. He explains the meaning and the purpose of his proposition: "When scientific analysis succeeds in bringing to light what it is that makes the work of art necessary — i.e. the informational formula, the generating principle, the raison d'être — it gives the artistic experience, and to pleasure that goes with it, its best justification, its richest food." His hefty volume combines "the invention of the artist's life" (published almost twenty years earlier), elements from the constitution of the literary field in the 19th century, considerations on Sartre, the total intellectual, on a Faulkner novel, on the *Quattrocento*; he says that in this way he is giving us the logic of the field of cultural production (try to apply *that*. . .) (see Chapter VI). On the basis of this knowledge that he has brought to us, he invites us to invent or re-invent a collective intellectual; intellectuals could work collectively in the defense of their own interests, to make the discourse of freedom heard.

This appeal does not seem to have been heeded; that must be why, forsaking his own field of production, he has moved his "critical power" to the unemployed and the activists fighting unemployment.

The Fortunes and Misfortunes of Professor Bourdieu

In *Pascalian Meditations*, Bourdieu expounds upon "the effects of scholastic isolation" (!), i.e. "an intellectual-centric distance with regard to the world". He writes, "Paradoxically, the social and mental rift is never seen so clearly as in the often pathetic and transitory attempts to fit into the real world, in particular through political engagement. . . whose irresponsible utopianism and unrealistic radicalness attest that this is just another way of denying the realities of the social world."[98]

This analysis applies exactly to the Bourdieu of today, who is definitely blind when it comes to himself. He has made himself the spokesman of the unemployed and he asks their "approval" to speak about their cause; he has retreated into militant, irresponsible, unrealistic and radical discourse. Acceptable if it were coming from those who suffer, from the lips of a Professor of the College of France it becomes demagoguic and untrue.

If, as Bourdieu affirms, "mass unemployment" is really "the most effective weapon available to employers for imposing stagnation or declining wages, the intensification of work effort, the degradation of work conditions, job insecurity, flexibility, the installation of new forms of domination and the dismantling of the labor code", one wonders why it took them so long to find this miraculous weapon. Are the employers so stupid? But isn't he concerned then, in revealing "the indisputable relation between the rate of unemployment and the rate of return", that employers will use this Bourdieusian discovery to their very great advantage, and even more broadly?[99] Having subordinated himself to the unemployed, Bourdieu set himself up a few days later as their advisor: he went to the École Normale, that they had taken over, and pointed out to them which places it would be most welcome, or necessary, to occupy, the Sciences Po school, for example.[100] We might shrug at his striking this pose, in itself, but when it applies to the drama of unemployment, it scandalizes me.

Some twenty years ago, Bourdieu said that he wrote to "prevent people from saying whatever they liked about the social world" (!). I write, he said, so that "the mouthpieces can no longer make noises that sound like words, concerning the social world". Since his words, the things that he said and kept saying, apparently were not being heard well enough, he started to make noise himself. And at that time he expressed the desire that the pundits, those speakers who usurp the public discourse, should set themselves the "task of working toward their own demise". And he added, to conclude the interview: "At least we can dream, for once..."[101]

Nobody never imagined or dreamed that Bourdieu, the

engaged intellectual, should work toward his own demise. . . One only wished that instead of inundating us with his theory, his conceptual ratiocinations and vast impractical programs, he would put his theory into practice ["a practice preserved in theory", "to take him at his word, betting that a science is possible that does not have the authority to elude reality"(!), as one of his faithful followers writes] [102]. In short, one could wish that Bourdieu would produce some results and also invest, in his engagements "in the most urgent causes", a bit of reflection — and consistency.

In *Critique*, in a special issue on "the paradigm that, for a good third of a century, has formed and informed our thoughts about the social",[103] one of Bourdieu's devotees spoke about "the astonishing stability" of "the scientific and political positions" taken by this "trajectory of the exception".[104] The stability of his scientific position? Certainly; and I would even say, a certain immobility (in spite of his reversal in regard to the State. . .). But stability in his political position, certainly not.

In May 1968, Bourdieu was discreet, one might even say absent. He has been reproached for that by the far Left. When people were talking about how the communist intellectuals prostrated themselves before "the party" and "the working class" in the Fifties, he was violently sarcastic; you would never have imagined that he would submit his prose to the service of the ranks of the unemployed in 1998.

In the High Mass of *Critique* — which I find lengthy, although it apologizes for being so short: only 160 pages — the master of ceremonies speaks of all the "diverse and important interlocutors" (?) that he had won over, "all over the world".[105] While he did, indeed, win over many people in scholarly circles, at least in France, in the post-Sixties period, that was mostly for two reasons: a great passion for work, even an exaltation of work, and an evident distance from engagement. The climate at the time was riven with indifference to work (that word is weak[106]) and fed up with engagement and an insane, fierce, and I must say, stupid politicization. It was the time when young Maoists wanted to make their heads empty vessels — and they succeeded. In those years Bourdieu's posture was rather uncommon, which gave him the ability to convince, to involve. Consecration (election to the College of France) might have enabled him to retain his sense of work but make him drop the febrility and the hasty approach to the empirical, and therefore to produce for real. And to also drop his proud self-assurance. Doesn't he find it funny to use as an epigraph, here and there (for example, in *The State Nobility*, p. 99), a bracing thought from Hegel: "As the old joke goes, 'When God gives someone a function, he also gives him competence'; nowadays, nobody would take that seriously." Alas!

Bourdieu takes it very seriously.

What Bourdieu thinks of his own work, deep in his heart, we do not know. That he is losing ground in France is certain, and he cannot possibly have failed to recognize it[107], the celebration in *Critique* notwithstanding. Abroad, on the other hand, he seems to go from success to success. His triumph in America is not surprising, since the French have always been "the providers of political-philosophical ideology pretending to universal applicability", as Raymond Aron noted in his criticism of Althusser; he also stressed that the Germans had lost their "philosophical fecundity".[108] And in Germany, too, Bourdieu seems to "go over" well enough: a conference on his work was held in Berlin in 1993. Pierre Bourdieu does, indeed, provide a *political-philosophical ideology pretending to universal applicability.*

The special issue of *Critique* advises us, "It is not by chance that several French and North American philosophers have made a point of participating in this issue. Bourdieu and philosophy, that is not a simple story. . . philosophers are more and more often reading Bourdieu as a philosopher. And not only for the brilliant background in traditional philosophy that he deploys in his books. It is because, very early on, he was able to take advantage of analytical philosophy (the Wittgenstein-Austin-Searle school), which French philosophy preferred to ignore for as long as possible."[109] Bourdieu is read by philosophers? Which ones?

Twenty years ago, Bourdieu put "philosophy" in its place. In one of the first issues of his *Actes de la recherche en sciences sociales*, he proudly committed "a crime of lese-majesty": the pieces featured in this special issue, "A Critique of the Scholarly Tradition", "take philosophy as their topic, a *dominant discipline* which, by tradition, sets the boundaries of the sciences, classifies and organizes them, and under its pretence of freedom, contributes in its own way to imposing order, and not only on science. We must be resolved: in order to survive, philosophy, which had been so high and mighty, exerting its dominion, must today proclaim its own death and, diluting itself in the social sciences, to try to dissolve". Saying that scientific criticism must sometimes take the form of criticism *ad hominem*, he then made a point of specifying that such criticism "does not aim to impose a new form of terrorism, but to make all forms of terrorism difficult".[110] [Reader, remember here Brecht's stage directions, and thus my own. . .].

His "iron fist" approach to philosophy — to paraphrase Michel Deguy — was extremely well received, especially when *Distinction* came out, in which Bourdieu brought down Derrida, "the last philosophical chimera", after having debunked Kant, Heidegger, etc..[111] [Since then, Derrida has been placed back on his pedestal]. A few years later, Bourdieu denied that this was a "denial" — saying that "denying" is not the same as "negating" (!) — to those "who see all sociological analysis of philosophical practices and institutions as 'an attack' against philosophy". He explained that social sciences require philosophy and that sociological analysis thus "serves" (and assists) "this long-dominant discipline".[112] [In 1983, it was no longer dominant]. His critiques, in his view, are always fair and scientific, as are his lessons. Philosophy must practice the reflexivity that he preaches, exhibits, practices, demands; in short, it must analyze "socially" its problems, its practices, its operation; therefore it must read Bourdieu, to learn from Bourdieu.

Now, Bourdieu turns toward philosophy once again. "Not a day goes by when I do not read or re-read philosophical works. . . . I am constantly working with philosophers and I am constantly challenging the philosophers to work."[113] Moreover, the editor behind the special issue in *Critique* says: "His references to Spinoza, Kant and Leibnitz are far from being simply decorative."[114] [Why would you write that? Is there a risk that we might have thought, or should I say, that we might have dared to think, such a thing?]

Very recently, he offered us his *Pascalian Meditations* (whose status, to tell the truth, is not clearly definable). He reminds us that he had kept philosophy at arm's length (partly because of his sojourn in Algeria), and of his dissatisfaction with the philosophical game; and he expresses, through Wittgenstein (for he wants to avoid sacrificing to confidence!) "[his] essential feelings in connection with philosophy". "What would be the use of studying philosophy, if all it does for you is to enable you to express yourself in a relatively plausible way on certain abstruse questions of logic, etc., and if it does not improve your way of thinking on the important questions of everyday life, if it does not make you more conscientious than a journalist, in using the dangerous expressions that people of that ilk use for their own ends?"[115] He is not a philosopher, but he is at least a cousin of philosophy. And then, with *The Weight of the World*, he gives us "another way of making politics". He really is giving us a political-philosophical ideology.

The new posture that Pierre Bourdieu has adopted as an engaged intellectual, and his new writings that waver between a somewhat pandering journalism and "the thoughtful thought", allow for a certain sterility in the sociology that proclaimed itself a science — and a science in the service of the dominated, claiming to give them "weapons". It is this sterility that we will now examine, going over his principle writings of the last twenty years; this sociology, which is useless for the dominated, leaves apprentice sociologists without real tools, abandoning them in a devastated battlefield.

In a recent interview, Bourdieu boldly and somewhat unconsciously affirmed, "It is often said that the scientist must take into account his own consciousness, his deontology or, as we say today, his 'ethics'. Actually, punishment is what he must take into account. In the end, crime is likely to be punished".[116] We are not really asking that much! Simply, Bourdieu should take professional criticism into account without calling it "resistance"; he should show concrete results in a defined field, rather than vaticinating between "criticism of (his) critics" as he does in *Pascalian Meditations*[117] and the unrealizable sociology of the universal, or leaning too far toward the political podium.

Footnotes

1. Pierre Bourdieu, "Le sociologue en question", in *Questions de sociologie*, Paris, Editions de Minuit, 1980, p. 41.
2. L. Trotsky's response to B. Suvarin (Constantinople, July 3, 1929) in: *A contre-courant, Ecrits 1925-1939,* Paris, Denoël, 1985, p. 276.
3. Céline, *Bagatelles pour un massacre,* Paris, Denoël, 1937, p. 27.
4. I read or re-read all of Pierre Bourdieu's books [except *The Political Ontology of Martin Heidegger*, 1988], many of his articles published in *Actes de la recherche* and in various other reviews for the period antedating the creation of *Actes*. I also read quite a few articles from *Actes* (which I had skimmed through regularly), always choosing them according to the title, and not according to who was the author. I can say, once and for all, that of course many very interesting articles are found there. [Let me add that I published seven articles there myself, in 1975, 1976, 1978, 1979, and 1981].
5. Bourdieu leads his followers to repeat experiments on falsely constructed subjects to prove the scientific quality of his statements; see, for example, "Salut littéraire et literature du salut. Deux trajectoires de romanciers catholiques: François Mauriac et Henry Bordeaux", *Actes de la recherche en sciences sociales,* No. 111-112, March 1996, pp. 36-58. (This note is not aimed against the author of the article, but against the "constructed" subject which clearly illustrates the sniggering superiority of Bourdieu's sociology.) On Marxism and its function of providing a "lazy security" ("it is so easy and comfortable to lock oneself up in a tradition"): "La sociologie est-elle une science?", interview with Pierre Thuillier, *La Recherche,* No. 112, June 1980, republished under the title: "Une science qui dérange [A disturbing science]", in *Questions de sociologie,* pp. 24-25.
6. Claude Grignon, "Le savant et le lettré ou l'examen d'une désillusion [The Scientist and the Well-read man or an Examination of a Disillusion]", *Revue européenne des sciences sociales* [*European Review of social sciences*], volume XXXIV, 1996, No. 103, p. 84; see the criticique of the *habitus*, pp. 96-98.
7. Michel Deguy, *Choses de la poésie et affaires culturelles,*

Paris, Hachette, 1986, pp. 122-151.

8. Méditations pascaliennes, Paris, le Seuil, 1997, p. 13. In my book, the reader will find exclamation points and question marks intended to attract or to awake the attention of the reader, for I fear that my quotations, essential but often tedious or difficult to comprehend, may lead the reader to read Bourdieu "distractedly". . . In this, I merely imitate Bertolt Brecht who, in *Petit organon,* recommended that the gestures be emphasized by "musical addresses to the public" or a change of lighting, or a new title. . . ("Petit organon pour le théâtre [A Little Organum for the Theatre]", *Théâtre populaire,* No. 11, January-February 1955, p. 13). The idea came to me, somewhat ironically, because Bourdieu's prose appears to me to be a sophisticated version (in writing) of a schematizing (abstracting) way of thinking, as was Brecht's.
9. Pierre Bourdieu, Excerpt from a talk given December 7, 1993 at the C.N.R.S., *Le Journal du C.N.R.S.,* No 50, February 1994.
10. Pierre Bourdieu, *Méditations pascaliennes, op. cit.,* p. 16.
11. Pierre Bourdieu, *Le Sens pratique*, Paris, Editions de Minuit, 1980, p. 30.
12. Pierre Bourdieu with Loïc J D. Wacquant, *Réponses. Pour une anthropologie réflexive*, Paris, Le Seuil, 1992, pp. 176-177.
13. *Ibid,* p. 181. Did Bourdieu really "betray" the École Normale? Is he any different from the alumni of the École Normale Superieure? In regard to the ENS's symbolic weakening, he wrote that students coming from privileged families "probably expected something from the ENS that it could not give, i.e. that which one would expect from a really powerful school" (pp. 301-302), and he added, in a footnote, at the "risk of causing a scandal": "I admit that I am inclined to think that the success of the ENS in the 1970's, the Leninist version of the phantasm of the philosopher-king could serve as a release system, albeit somewhat unexpected, for the socially made up 'will for power' that the 'Normaliens' brought into the institution. . . " *La Noblesse d'État, Grandes écoles et esprit de corps*, Paris, Editions de Minuit, 1989, p. 302, note 38.
14. This idea is remarkably well developed by David Shahar, in *Le Palais des vases brisés*; when I read it several years ago, I

copied it and put it up on my office wall, without any citation. The sentence can be found in one of the first three volumes; I did not have time to relocate the page.

15. Jacques Prentki, Collège de France, *Leçon inaugurale,* April 23, 1965 (Chaire de Physique théorique des particules élémentaires [Chair of Theoretical Physics of Elementary Particles), p. 8.
16. Lucien Febvre, "Vivre l'histoire" (1941), *Combats pour l'histoire,* Paris, rééd., Armand Colin, 1992, p. 21.
17. *Le Sens pratique, op. cit.,* p. 40, note 31.
18. Pierre Bourdieu, "L'art de résister aux paroles", interview with Didier Eribon, *Libération,* November 3 and 4 1979, republished in *Questions de sociologie, op. cit.,* p. 13.
19. Pierre Bourdieu, "Où sont les terroristes ?", *Esprit,* November-December 1980 ("piss-copy of the episcopate", p. 254). On the use of "la thèse et la foutaise [theses and faces]", see, for example: "La grande illusion des intellectuels", Interview with Didier Eribon, *Le Monde Dimanche,* May 4, 1980, republished under the title "Comment libérer les intellectuels libres? [How to free the free intellectuals?] in *Questions de sociologie, op. cit.*, p. 73, and *La Distinction, critique sociale du jugement*, Paris, Editions de Minuit, 1979, p. 598.
20. Pierre Bourdieu, "Le sociologue en question", in *Questions de sociologie, op. cit.,* p. 39.
21. Pierre Bourdieu, "L'ontologie politique de Martin Heidegger", *Actes de la recherche en sciences sociales*", November 1975, Nos 5-6, p. 119.
22. Pierre Bourdieu, with Hans Haacke, *Libre-échange*, Paris, Le Seuil/Les Presses du réel, 1994, p. 110.
23. "Le sociologue en question", *article cit.,* p. 49.
24. *Libre-échange, op. cit.,* p. 9.
25. Pierre Bourdieu, "Le marché linguistique", Exposé given at the University of Geneva, December 1978, *Questions de sociologie, op. cit.,* p. 131.
26. *Libre-échange, op. cit.*.
27. Jean-Pierre Martin, *Contre Céline,* Paris, José Corti, 1997, p. 64. The comparison between Céline and Bourdieu has been waiting on my mind for quite some time, hounding me. I therefore read, a little randomly, some recent books on Céline; this one in particular gives a good analysis of Céline's personality, and helped me "to understand" the conduct of the

Bourdieu character.

28. Pierre Bourdieu, "Fieldwork in philosophy", *Choses dites,* Paris, Editions de Minuit, 1987, p. 42. The entire passage is worth reading: "Reducing the amount of time and energy devoted to *show* means that the technical output must be increased considerably; but, in a universe where the social definition of the practice implies a measure of *show*, of *epideixis* as the pre-Socratics said (who recognized themselves), it also means exposing oneself to the loss of the symbolic profit of recognition which is associated with the normal exercise of mental activity. This has as a counterpart the fact that any concession, even the most limited and most controlled, to *show business* (which has more and more become part of the trade of the intellectual) entails risks of all kinds" (pp. 41-42).
29. Méditations pascaliennes, *op. cit.,* p. 15.
30. Cf. Jean-Pierre Martin, *Contre Céline, op. cit.,* pp. 63-79.
31. Loïc J.D. Wacquant, Presentation and Introduction to *Réponses. Pour une anthropologie réflexive, op. cit.,* pp. 7-42.
32. *Libre-échange, op. cit.,* p. 59.
33. "Comment libérer les intellectuels libres", *article cit.,* p. 71 and p. 70.
34. *Ibid,* p. 76.
35. Méditations pascaliennes, *op. cit.,* p. 16.
36. *On Sur la télévision,* Paris, Liber-Raisons d'agir, 1997, p. 12.
37. *Addition:* Pierre Bourdieu has just published this harangue to the railwaymen. He defined (imagined) the meaning of the railwaymen's strike: "I am here to give my support to all those who have been fighting, for three weeks, against the destruction of *a civilization,* associated with the existence of a public utility, that of republican equality of rights, the right to education, health, culture, research, art, and, above all, to work." "Contre la destruction d'une civilisation", *Contre-feux,* Paris, Liber-Raisons d'agir, 1998, p. 30.
38. *Libre-échange, op. cit.,* p. 38.
39. *Les Règles de l'art,* Genèse et structures du champ littéraire, Paris, le Seuil, 1994, p. 462.
40. Pierre Bourdieu, "Ce que parler veut dire", A presentation to the congress of the AFEF, Limoges, October 30, 1977, printed in *Le français d'aujourd'hui,* 41, March 1978, and suppl. to No 41, republished in *Questions de sociologie, op. cit.,* p. 110.

41. Nathalie Heinich, "A propos de l'exposition Watteau", *Actes de la recherche en sciences sociales,* No 59, September 1985, p. 94.
42. Ines Champey, "A propos de l'exposition Watteau: une réponse", *Actes de la recherche en sciences sociales,* No 60, October 1985, p. 89. "How can we leave hanging and between parentheses a means of objectively verifying the assumption that seems to take the place of a conclusion (finding out whether Watteau did *indeed have* any trouble selling all his works), . . . " This unbridled criticism was followed by a (vast) program: "Isn't it the job of the sociologist to analyze the effect of the exhibition itself and the symbolic violence that it achieves today, while clearly distinguishing the contemporary exhibition from what really occurred in the painter's life and which only a solid work by a historian (taking account of the conceptual and methodological discoveries of sociology) can properly try to reconstitute?"
43. Pierre Bourdieu, "Une science qui dérange", *article cit.,* pp. 21-22.
44. Pierre Bourdieu, *Avant-propos dialogue*, a foreword to : Jacques Maître, *L'autobiographie d'un paranoïaque*, Paris, Anthropos, 1994, p. XIV.
45. *Réponses. Pour une anthropologie réflexive, op. cit.,* p. 193.
46. *Libre-échange, op. cit.,* p. 100.
47. Marc Bloch — Lucien Febvre, *Correspondance,* I, (1928-1933), Paris, Fayard, 1994.
48. Harold Rosenberg, *La Tradition du nouveau*, Paris, Editions de Minuit, 1962, [the chapter that I use here is entitled "Les héros de la science marxiste", pp. 177-196].
49. *Leçon sur la leçon*, Leçon inaugurale, Collège de France, Sociology chair, April 23, 1982, Paris, Editions de Minuit, 1982, p. 6.
50. Harold Rosenberg, *La Tradition du nouveau, op. cit.,* p. 177.
51. Méditations pascaliennes, *op. cit.,* p. 15.
52. Pierre Bourdieu, *Esquisse d'une théorie de la pratique,* Genève/Paris, Droz, 1972, p. 155.
53. *Leçon sur la leçon, op. cit.,* p. 13. On "the law", Bourdieu says elsewhere: "Publicizing laws that presuppose *laissez-faire*. . . extends the domain of liberty. A law that is unknown is [experienced as] a nature, a destiny (such is the case of the relationship between inherited cultural capital and school suc-

cess); a law that is known seems like the possibility of a freedom". He is then asked, "Isn't it dangerous to talk of laws?" He answers: "Yes, certainly. And I avoid doing so as much as possible." "Le sociologue en question", *Questions de sociologie, op. cit.*, p. 45.

54. In *Méditations pascaliennes, op. cit.*, p. 16, Bourdieu takes on the "malevolent" and the "those who don't see clearly". To let you in on the laugh, I will give you his definitions: "The decreased status of this pariah science inclines and allows those who do not see clearly to think that they are beyond something that is sometimes beyond them and the malevolent to produce a deliberately reductive image without incurring the sanctions normally attached to overly flagrant abuses of the 'principle of charity'" (!) On the subject of truths that one does not like to hear: *Cf*, for example, Pierre Bourdieu, "Une science qui dérange", *art. cit.*.
55. *Leçon sur la leçon, op. cit.*, p. 16.
56. *Méditations. . . , op. cit.,* p. 16.
57. David Shub, cit. by Harold Rosenberg, *La Tradition du nouveau,, op. cit.*, p. 183.
58. *Sur la télévision, op. cit.,* p. 36.
59. I read the following "Inaugural Lessons" (in chronological order): George Dumézil (Indo-European Civilization, 1949), Fernand Braudel (History of modern civilization, 1949), Rene Huyghe (Physiology of the visual arts, 1951), Gaston Wiet (Arab language and literature, 1951), Martial Guéroult (History and technology of philosophical systems, 1951), Andre Pézard (Italian literature and civilization, 1951), Louis Chevalier (Social history and structures of Paris and the Paris area, 1951), Henri-Charles Puech (History of the religions, 1952), Henri Laoust (Moslem sociology, 1956), Robert Minder (Languages and literatures of Germanic origin, 1958), Claude Lévi-Strauss (Anthropology elementary particles, 1965), François Jacob (Cellular genetics, 1965), George Blin (Modern French literature, 1966), Jacques Monod (Molecular biology, 1967), Paul Lemerle (History and civilization of Byzantium, 1967), André Leroi-Gourhan (Prehistory, 1969), Raymond Aron (Sociology of modern civilization, 1970), Michel Foucault (History of the systems of thought, 1970), Georges Duby (History of medieval societies, 1970), Pierre-Gilles de Gennes (Physics of condensed matter, 1971), Em-

manuel Le Roy Ladurie (History of modern civilization, 1973), Jacques-Louis Lions (Modern mathematical analysis, 1975), Julian de Ajuriaguerra (Neuropsychology of development, 1976), Roland Barthes (Literary semiology, 1977), Jean-Marie Lehn (Chemistry of molecular interactions, 1980), Yves Bonnefoy (Comparative studies of poetic function, 1981). This choice is quite arbitrary; many famous lecturers are absent, but this long and often enthralling cavalcade seemed to me sufficient for better appreciating the approach taken by Pierre Bourdieu.

60. *Pour une anthropologie réflexive, op. cit.,* p. 176.
61. Pierre Bourdieu, "Il faudrait réinventer une sorte d'intellectuel collectif sur le modèle de ce qu'ont été les Encyclopédistes [We should reinvent a kind of collective intellectual, on the model of what the Encyclopédistes were]", remarks recorded by Franck Nouchi, *Le Monde,* December 7, 1993.
62. Hume, cit. by Pierre Bourdieu, Monique de Saint Martin, "Le patronat [Employers]", *Actes de la recherche en sciences sociales,*", No 20-21, March-April 1978, p. 3.
63. *Méditations pascaliennes, op. cit.,* p. 292, note 2 of Chapter II.
64. *Pour une anthropologie réflexive, op. cit.,* p. 86.
65. *Ibid,* p. 87.
66. *Ibid,* p. 90.
67. Pierre Bourdieu, "La démission de l'État [the abdication of the State]", in *La Misère du monde,* Paris, le Seuil, 1993, quotations extracted pp. 219-222.
68. "Pierre Bourdieu, Notre État de misère [Our State of misery]", interview conducted by Sylvaine Pasquier, *L'Express,* March 16, 1993.
69. Pierre Bourdieu, "Effets de lieu", in *La Misère du monde, op. cit.,* p. 159.
70. V. note 68.
71. *La Noblesse d'État, op. cit.,* p. 118, note 11.
72. "Esprits d'État. Genèse et structure du champ bureaucratique [Spirits of State. Genesis and structure of the bureaucratic field]", (1991), in: *Raisons pratiques,* Paris, le Seuil, 1994, p. 131.
73. "Esprits d'État. Genèse et structure. . .", *op. cit.,* p. 101 and p. 102.

In addition: A speech published in *Contre-feux* that Pierre Bourdieu gave to an audience of Greek trade unionists shows how . . . flexible his thinking was with regard to the State. Let us consider a few assertions. The United States "is kind of a fulfillment of the dream of the dominant, a State that (as Loïc Wacquant has shown) is reduced more and more to its police function" (p. 37). Referring to the beginnings of the State in England and France, he says: "The State, as it advances, acquires autonomy, becomes partially independent of the dominant social and economic forces" (p. 38) and he denounces "the process of regression of the State" in Europe (p. 38) for he is *for* the State, he defends it. "The State is an ambiguous reality. One cannot be satisfied to say that it is a tool in the service of the dominant. Certainly, the State is not completely neutral, completely independent of the dominant, but its autonomy becomes all the greater as it grows older, as it becomes more powerful, as it encompasses within its structures the more important social achievements, etc.." "To resist the *involution of the State,* i.e. regressing toward a penal State, . . . and sacrificing the social functions little by little, . . . the social movement can find support on the part of those in charge of the social welfare administration, . . . who are opposed to the bean-counters . . ." (p. 39). "I think that the dominated may find it beneficial to defend the state, in particular in its social aspect. This defense of the State is not inspired by nationalism. While one may fight against the national State, it should be defended for its *universal* functions, which it fills and which can be filled as well, if not better, by a supranational state" (pp. 46-47). "Historically, the State was a force of rationalization, but it was put to the service of the dominant forces. To keep that from happening, . . . a new internationalism should be invented, at least at the regional scale of Europe. . . We should build institutions that could control the forces of the financial market, to introduce — the Germans have a splendid word — *Regrezionsverbot,* a prohibition of regression in regard to the social protection that has been achieved across Europe" (p. 47). "The myth of 'globalization' and the European social state", a speech before the General Confederation of Greek workers, in Athens, in October 1996, *Contre-feux, op. cit.,* pp. 34-50.

74. *La Noblesse d'État, op. cit.,* p. 14.

75. Christiane Chauviré, "Avant-Propos", special issue, Pierre Bourdieu, *Critique,* No. 579-580, August-September 1995, p. 547.
76. *Les Héritiers*, Les étudiants et la culture, Paris, Editions de Minuit, 1964, p. 115.
77. *La Reproduction*, Eléments pour une théorie du système de l'enseignement, Paris, Editions de Minuit, 1970, p. 253 and p. 254. I should mention that Bourdieu, who for thirty years had been pronouncing one incontrovertible verdict, as stated in *Reproduction,* now says that school produces contradictory effects — on young immigrants, for example. Cf. "La démission de l'État", in *La Misère du monde, op. cit.*, pp. 223-226 ("l'école des sous-prolétaires [school for the sub-proletariat]").
78. *Pour une anthropologie réflexive, op. cit.,* p. 47.
79. *Ibid,* p. 46.
80. *La Noblesse d'État, op. cit.,* p. 123.
81. *Ibid.,* pp. 163-164.
82. *Ibid.,* p. 533.
83. "Méthode scientifique et hiérarchie sociale des objets", *Actes de la recherche en sciences sociales,* No. 1, 1975, p. 4.
84. "Espace social et champ du pouvoir", *Raisons pratiques, op. cit.,* p. 57.
85. "Reproduction interdite. La dimension symbolique de la domination économique", *Etudes rurales,* No 113-114, January-June 1989, p. 35, note 22.
86. *Pour une anthropologie réflexive, op. cit.,* p. 70.
87. "Méthode scientifique et hiérarchie sociale des objets", *art. cit.,* p. 6.
88. Pierre Bourdieu with Yvette Delsaut, "Le couturier et sa griffe – contribution à une théorie de la magie [Designers and labels — contribution to a theory of magic]", *Actes de la recherche en sciences sociales,* No 1, January 1975, pp. 7-36.
89. Pierre Bourdieu (under the direction of), *Un art moyen,* Essai sur les usages sociaux de la photographie, Paris, Editions de Minuit, 1965, p. 138.
90. Pierre Bourdieu, "Le sociologue en question", *art. cit.,* p. 51.
91. This study included the museums of Madrid, Barcelona, Athens, Delphi, Nauplie, Milan, Bologna, Amsterdam, The Hague, Poznan, Lublin, Warsaw, Cracow, Lodz; Agen, Arles, Arras, Autun, Bourg-en-Bresse, Colmar, Dieppe, Dijon,

Douai, Dreux, Laon, Lille, Louviers, Lyon, Marseilles, Mills, Pau, Rouen, Tours, Paris. When you see the results, this list seems astonishingly broad. Or vice versa.

92. Pierre Bourdieu and Alain Darbel, with Dominique Schnapper, *L'Amour de l'art*, Les musées d'art européens et leur public, Paris, Editions de Minuit, 1969 p. 166, p. 165 and p. 164.
93. Pierre Bourdieu, "La pensée Tietmeyer", a talk given at the Franco-German Cultural Meetings, University of Freiburg, October 1996, *Contre-feux, op. cit.,* 1998, p. 52.
94. *La Distinction, op. cit.,* p. 448.
95. *Ibid.,* p. 432.
96. *Pour une anthropologie réflexive, op. cit.,* p. 56.
97. *Les Règles de l'art, op. cit.,* p. 14.
98. *Méditations pascaliennes, op. cit.,* p. 53.
99. Pierre Bourdieu, Frederic Lebaron, Gerard Mauger, "Les actions des chômeurs flambent", *Le Monde,* January 17, 1998.
100. *Le Nouvel Observateur,* January 22-28, 1998, Agathe Logeart, "Leçon de misère pour les normaliens [Lesson of misery for people from the Ecole Normale Superieure]": "Pierre Bourdieu came to lend his support, obligingly had an article distributed under the windows of the school, an article that he had had printed in that day's *Le Monde* newspaper; and he whispered into the microphones, which he affects to hate, that *'The first achievement of the movement is its very existence.'* Perched on the roofs, the invaders from Ulm did not hear any of the emphatic declarations of the sociologist who ended his peroration on '*the hypocrisy of the court trade unionism and the pretences of the socialist old boys from the ENA',* before advising that they take over the Sciences Po school and the ENA, '*those places where the government's blindness to the governed is born".* (p. 53).

    In addition: Bourdieu has published his impromptu speech from the time when the unemployed had a sit-in at the Advanced Teacher Training school [École Normale], January 17, 1998: "Le mouvement des chômeurs, un miracle social", in *Contre-feux, op. cit.,* pp. 102-104. "The scientific militant" stated his "admiration" and his "gratitude" for this "social miracle" of which "one will not immediately be able to discover all the virtues and benefits".
101. "L'art de résister aux paroles", *art. cit.,* p. 18.

102. Louis Pinto, "La théorie en pratique", *Critique,* special issue, Pierre Bourdieu, *op. cit.,* p. 620.
103. Christiane Chauviré, "Avant-propos", *Critique, op. cit.,* p. 547.
104. Gilbert Mauger, "L'engagement sociologique", *Critique, op. cit.,* p. 694.
105. V note 103.
106. In an interview with Jean-Claude Bringuier (1981), Fernand Braudel said that "the revolution of 1968" "had devalued the concept of work" [reported by: Pierre Daix, *Braudel,* Paris, Flammarion, 1995, p. 430]. The word seems appropriate to me, for the climate of that time. At least, I did feel that way.
107. *Le Monde* published a letter from a reader (L. Gruel) on April 17, 1998 responding to Bourdieu's article "Pour une gauche de gauche [For a left of the left]": "The article's only merit is that it testifies to the opinion of Pierre Bourdieu, an opinion that was summarized by a snarl of offhand judgments and 'mass-produced' indignations. I am not aware that Pierre Bourdieu has conducted the least study on the incidence, economic and social, of any particular political strategy or another, on the relationship between jobs, and length of employment, on the factors influencing the right-wing vote. Simplistic as I may be, I am thus inclined to think that his opinion on these questions is worth neither more nor less than that of any other celebrity, Yvette Horner or Raymond Poulidor, for example. . . I wonder what madness led Bourdieu to write such an article, what logic prompted *Le Monde* to publish it and especially why the groups most confronted with social violence could be supposed to have wished to see their suffering and revolts thus cloaked with sententious ignorance and frivolous self-satisfaction. . ."
    Libération published a letter from a reader (M. Gomez) on April 23, 1998, protesting against the article (yet another) on Bourdieu, and he delivered an opinion that reflects what is heard more and more frequently: "Is there anything else, apart from that (i.e., rage against neoliberalism) in the professor's mind, any idea at all, just one? We are always rehashing the great catalogue of universal whinging and whining."
108. Raymond Aron, *Marxismes imaginaires. D'une sainte famille à l'autre [Imaginary Marxisms. From one holy family to another],* Paris, Gallimard, 1970, p. 194. ("Althusser ou la

lecture pseudo-structuraliste de Marx.")

109. Christiane Chauviré, "Des philosophes lisent Bourdieu. Bourdieu/Wittgenstein : la force de l'habitus", *Critique, op. cit.,* p. 548.
110. Pierre Bourdieu (signed: Actes de la recherche), Preliminary, *Actes de la recherche en sciences sociales,* Nos 5-6, November 1975.
111. Michel Deguy, *Choses de la poésie . . . , op. cit.,* p. 123.
112. Pierre Bourdieu, "Les sciences sociales et la philosophie", *Actes de la recherche en sciences sociales,* Nos 47-48, June 1983, p. 45.
113. Pierre Bourdieu, *Pour une anthropologie réflexive, op. cit.,* p. 133.
114. Christiane Chauviré, "Des philosophes lisent Bourdieu. . .", *art. cit.,* p. 549.
115. *Méditations pascaliennes, op. cit.,* p. 53. This text had already been printed, in large font, in a whole page in *La Misère du monde, op. cit.,* p. 940.
116. Pierre Bourdieu, "Il faudrait réinventer une sorte d'intellectuel collectif. . . [We should reinvent a kind of collective intellectual. . .]" , *interview cit.*.
117. *Méditations pascaliennes, op. cit.,* "Digression. Critique de mes critiques", pp. 75-80.

Chapter I

Art And Manner
or
Manner and Art

Let's start by taking a look at a set of specific characteristics of Pierre Bourdieu's writings. These characteristics partly explain why his sociology inspires criticism: an ideological discourse clothed in intimidating rhetoric and a whole panoply of scientific pageantry.

His books of sociology and meta-sociology continually confer the leading role upon the *modus operandi*, justify his use of artificial language, go on at length about the sociologist's difficulties (i.e. all the "effort" his work required, and all his vexations in transmitting his knowledge, therefore a criticism of his critics — or his readers, including a preemptive criticism of any faulty readings. . .). They give an imperialist view of social science and an imaginative concept of the exact sciences, and systematically focus on the prosaic, the commonplace, which often entails a lack of clear linkage between comments that are precise and torrential and the general problem that Bourdieu says he is explicating for us.

He bases his rhetoric on an accumulation of details, as if that were a guarantee of scientific quality; but many of the details that he describes contribute nothing. Where Bourdieu obsessively reiterates his fixation with rigor, the reader generally sees manias and eccentricities that the sociologist thinks he can impose as scientific — just through repetition. A good look at a few quotations, selected from among a great many equivalent pages illustrating these constant features of Bourdieu's work, make one wonder about his definition of science.

Complaining (as he so often does) of the misunderstandings between the sociologist and his readers, Bourdieu has proposed that the primary cause of the poor transmission of his results lies in the fact that readers have only "a very approximate idea of the conditions of production of the discourse"; they retain "the theses", "the conclusions", "independently of the approach that produced them".[1] He thinks that it is essential to know *the manner* by which the sociologist works, in order to understand the results — although he does not explain why that would be so. "Knowledge of the conditions by which the result is produced, in all rigor approach, is one of the conditions of a rational communication of the conclusions of social science. The readers deal with finished products, which are presented to them in a different order from that in which they were discovered. . . What circulates between the scientist and the non-specialist, or even between the specialists in one science and in other sciences, . . . what is conveyed by the great organs of publicity are, at best, results, but never operations."[2]

No (hard) science has ever said that, "in all rigor", it had to show the "actual film of research" before presenting its results. This astonishing characteristic of social science must be justified for the reader who knows that, in physics or biology, the conditions of how a result was reached play only an anecdotal role in their exposition. For example, you don't have to read *The Double Helix* (James D. Watson, 1968) before you can learn the basics of molecular biology. While he is very emphatic about this thesis, Bourdieu is unable to explain why the finished product must not obscure the operations, must not obscure *the manner* in which the sociologist works, etc..

The conditions of production take up considerable space in Bourdieu's written *œuvre*, and reading it requires "technical" training and immense patience. However, in the prologue of a collection of speeches, *Sociology in Question* (from which I draw most of the quotations that follow), Bourdieu says: "Sociology would not be worth an hour's time, if it were just an expert's field of knowledge, reserved to the expert."[3] Another time, he deplores that "those in whose interest it would be" to adapt what the sociologist says, "do not have the instruments of appropriation (theoretical culture, etc.)".[4] Therefore, to read Bourdieu, he acknowledges, you need to have instruments of appropriation, you need to be an expert, despite his having said that he would not like to devote one hour to sociology if it were a body of knowledge for experts alone, etc.. And you have to be an expert all the more so since (as I have stressed) Bourdieu irrepressibly insists on the need for the complexity of his language, and he relentlessly justifies it.

> Bourdieu reminds us, nonstop, that coining new words, an "artificial language", *is required* in order to break with the assumptions and presuppositions of ordinary language, with the "naive projections of common meanings".[5] [Before we follow him on that trajectory, let us remind ourselves, and out to him, that in *Reproduction* (1970) — a collaborative work, it is true — the foreword suggests that he will avoid "taking the unreasonable course of coining an artificial language" (p. 10). Very soon, however, Bourdieu takes "the unreasonable course of coining a language. . . etc.", and he sticks to it. Ah, you have to be "an expert" to read it. . .]
>
> To *adequately construct the object of the study*, you have to break with the pre-constructions of ordinary language,

even if Bourdieu acknowledges that scientific analysis can be "rough, even laborious".[6] I admit that, when I stumbled across "the built-in structures of anticipation" while reading *Homo Academicus* (p. 117), I found that rough going. And I heartily approve the author when, in "The Literary Field", he admits the "ponderousness and ugliness of writing". True, he did warn us that he was "constrained" to it (!). All his long paraphrases are "essential" in order "to break with the routines of ordinary thought and perception". Thus, I find — and certainly you will find — that it is quite long to write (or to say) "the occupants of temporally dominated positions in the field of power", but it is ES-SEN-TIAL to construct the object sci-en-tif-ic-al-ly[7]... Imagine what would have happened if you had merely said "intellectuals", even with the quotation marks. [This said, reader, have some fun: ask your friends to give an example of "occupants of temporally dominated positions, etc.", and you will be astonished by the diversity of the answers.] As for "the built-in structures of anticipation", you will have understood, for you are a reader of Bourdieu, that we are talking about expectations...

Throughout his work, he has underscored the absolute need for "the complexity of a discourse which endeavors to match *the complexity of the object*" that it describes.[8]

All the complications that he imposes on the reader are necessary, *to prevent misreadings*. ". . . the difficulty of the style often derives from all the nuances, all the corrections, all the warnings, not to mention the repeated definitions and principles, which are necessary so that the discourse will carry within itself all possible defenses against distortion and embezzlement."[9] Embezzlement! [is the word adequate here? Isn't this grave sin usually inspired by cupidity, as the *Robert* dictionary says? To hell with readers like that!]

Much less frequently, it is true, Pierre Bourdieu has also said that he has tried to produce messages "*on several levels*", to be read by a "broad audience", the "general public", not to be cut off from them. A message on several levels is what he tries to present in *Actes de la recherche*, "by trying to express an analysis (that of haute couture, for example) in two ways: by photographs (organized according to a certain structure) and by analytical text". He goes on to say that "one can do that in a very general way".[10] He thinks he can thus escape both the complexity of the message and the difficulties of transmitting it. I have already given this example, for I think it is a glaring instance of the superficiality of "the scientist" — or his blindness. The "dominated", who have no "instruments of appropriation", will look at the photographs, i.e. they will have an analysis on a certain level. . . which Bourdieu seems to think is sufficient. Thus, his works seek the "general public", but although he usually repeats his definitions many times over, this time, he's forgotten to define "general public". Generally, he stresses that he has in mind the dominated (it is true that, by sheer number, they make up a "broad audience"), and that he wants to arm them. Perhaps sociology, by revealing the mechanisms by which the power has founded its effectiveness, provides a "means of dominating domination".[11] At once, you must object: how are these dominated folks, deprived of the instruments of appropriation, deprived of "cultural competence", of "theoretical culture", supposed to understand? How can they receive the means of dominating domination and of making use of it? Who can help them?

Bourdieu knows (and he recalls it in the prologue of *Questions of Sociology*) that one cannot count "on the bosses, the bishops or the journalists" to reveal the results of this sociology which exposes the hidden keys of their domination.[12] Perhaps you think that the dominant ones will be able to use these results to obscure even further, to dissimulate still better, the hidden sources of their power — for they have the instruments of appropriation (see their various types of capital, and don't forget the various states of those various types[13].).

Can science (criticism) be used by the dominant? No, for Bourdieu also says that "the better sociology fulfills its proper scientific function, the more likely it is to disappoint or to oppose the powers. This function is not to be used for something, i.e. by some one. . . its scientific function is to understand the social world, starting with power. And that is an operation which is not socially neutral and which certainly serves a social function. Among other reasons, because there is no power that does not owe some part (and not the least part) of its effectiveness to ignorance of the mechanisms by which it is founded".[14]

Two words are fundamental, even crucial, when reading Bourdieu. In terms of the reader, the word is "resistance"; "the logic behind this resistance and the ways in which it is manifested are completely analogous to the forms of resistance encountered by psychoanalytical discourse".[15] When it comes to the scholar, the word is "defenses". "You know, when I write, I fear many things. . . I try to forestall misreadings, and often I can foresee them. But the little warnings that I slip between parentheses, quotation marks, brackets, etc., only reach those who do not need them."[16] In short, the scene is set: there are readers who are rigidly resistant, because they do not want to be "disturbed" by "a science that is disturbing" — "because it reveals things that are hidden and sometimes covered up, like the correlation between success in school. . . and social origin or, better yet, the family's inherited cultural capital";[17] on the other side stands the scholar, girded with defenses in order to avoid being misread, misunderstood, subjected to "inattentive readings".[18] And who, in spite of that, after more than thirty years of enormous, furious effort, etc., of ceaselessly publishing results and "prescriptions", has acknowledged: "I have indeed the feeling that I am rather poorly understood."[19] [This brings to mind the readers' reactions, excuse me, their resistance! For example, the first chapter of *Homo Academicus*, "A Book to be Burned?" No, no, for this is his expression; to the ordinary reader, a sociology book is readable and usable, or simply to be closed and put back on the shelf]. How can he be understood, when he has willfully made himself illegible, to avoid misreadings?

Compared to the "loudspeakers", i.e. the politicians, journalists, and pundits, Bourdieu says that scholarly discourse "has everything against it: the difficulty and slowness of its elaboration, which often means it arrives after the battle is over; its inevitable complexity, which discourages simplistic or prejudiced minds or, simply, those who do not have the cultural capital necessary to decipher it; its abstract impersonal quality. . . and, especially, the distance from generally accepted ideas and prior convictions."[20] You read that right: the complexity of the speech discourages minds "that do not have the cultural capital necessary to decipher it". What an admission and what a contradiction!

But this contradiction is followed by another, also sizeable. Bourdieu affirms that there is a gap between his results and the generally accepted ideas and prior convictions; he repeats that "assumptions must be shaken"[21] and, he says, somewhat bitterly, that what is "unforgivable" in the sociologist (the scientist) "is that he hands over to every comer the secrets that had been reserved to the initiated".[22] Bourdieu seems to read his own works "poorly" (or inattentively?), for he speaks of the "secrets" that he makes available to us, and at another time he affirms, "Part of a social scientist's work consists in discovering everything that is both hidden and revealed by ordinary language. This means that one is exposing oneself to being reproached for stating the obvious or, worse, for laboriously retranslating, in a ponderously conceptual language, the basic truths of common sense or intuition that are at the same time more subtly and more pleasantly presented by the moralists and novelists."[23] So, are the "secrets" that he "gives" us "statements of the obvious" or "basic truths"? In fact, reading Bourdieu, one rather often finds generally accepted ideas newly translated into a ponderously conceptual language; many of his writings, off-putting and pedantic as they are, state what is already known. It is true that he has also said that scientific discourse "generally arrives after the battle is over", in short, much ado about nothing... Then, in what sense is this a disturbing science? [Then again, you may recall that he *also* said that he is giving us "secrets", etc., "the least expected thing, the most improbable"[24]...]

Reading these last pages, you must have become impatient over all the contradictions, the reversals that are being inflicted on you, but it is impossible to read or critique Bourdieu without being obliged to follow the meanderings of his assertions. His assurance is never shaken by his contradictions and his inconsistencies — which may be one more "reason" he has for justifying the need for a "complex" language.

The collection *Sociology in Question* tries to escort us into "the laboratories of science", to make us masters of a method of thinking. There's nothing new here; in fact, he takes up again what was already expounded at length in the books where his "results" are published: reflections on method, concepts indefatigably defined (field, capital, *habitus*), philosophical problems posed anew by scientific sociology, i.e. metaphysical problems transformed into problems "susceptible to being dealt with scientifically, therefore politically".[25] [Are we to understand that major problems of mechanics, such as, for example, the stability of a bridge, the holding power of a dam, being governed scientifically, are also open to being governed politically?] It is a pity that Bourdieu does not define and does not even hesitate over the meaning of "*politically*".

Although he says that if the sociologist has a role, "it would be to give weapons rather than to teach lessons",[26] Bourdieu teaches many lessons and gives many "opinions", some of which clarify the inflated concept that he has of social science and the imaginative concept that he has of science. Affirming that he rejects the idea of sociological imperialism, he says that every science must, "with its own means, account for the greatest possible number of things, including things which apparently or really are explained by other sciences".[27] There again, the word "really" makes the proposition debatable. Would anyone say, for example, that quantum mechanics should explain things that are "really explained" by chemistry? Rather, it deals with things that are not. But scientific sociology must explain things that are already explained, without Bourdieu saying why.

His concept of the scientific nature of sociology translates, in his work, into a superabundance of details and examples, as if their proliferation would take on value of evidence, and as if the automatic repetition of the opinions that he spews were enough to make them attain the status of scientific truths. The repetitions in Bourdieu's books (repetitions that terrorize by stupefying, or that sound an alarm) express what it is that he wants. "The dominant is the one who has the means of imposing on the dominated that he perceive him the way he demands to be perceived."[28] By his repetitions, by his assured tone, by his jargon, Bourdieu seeks to impose his truth on us. "As soon as there is a social space, there is struggle; there is a struggle for domination, there is a dominant pole, there is a dominated pole, and from that moment onward, there are antagonistic truths. No matter what we do, the truth is antagonistic. If there is one truth, it is that the truth is the result of a battle."[29]

In his effort to impose himself, to dominate, Bourdieu affirms that *everything* has a meaning, a meaning that he knows how to decipher. For example, a grammatical slip supposedly made by Valéry Giscard d'Estaing is interpreted thus: his "hypo-correction" was only possible "because the person who transgressed the rule. . . proclaimed, by other aspects of his language — pronunciation, for example — and also by everything that he is, by everything that he does, that he *could* speak correctly".[30] His books are full of equally shocking observations and results.

What is unique in Bourdieu's "theoretical practice" is that it is applied feverishly to a multitude of minor topics, and that it leaves the big questions aside. It is easier to talk about the museum-going public than to talk about art, or the crisis of liturgy rather than religion; it is easier to reduce human behaviors to interests ("sociology cannot get by without the axiom of interest, understood as the individual *investment in the game*, which is both a condition and a product of membership in a field") and to strategies ("the unconscious relation between a *habitus* and a field"[31]), rather than to question them and join in the subtle "intuitions" of the novelists.

He states that "one of the secrets of the sociologist's

trade consists in knowing how to come up with empirical topics about which one can really pose very general questions". For example, by looking at the relationship between the popular classes and photography, you can tackle the question of realism and formalism in art, a question which, at times, has became a political question.[32] Here, Bourdieu is trying to impose on us the idea that by illuminating a problem in the sociology of art (formalism) by a marginal problem from the sociology of the popular classes, he is producing decisive results. We are still waiting for the breakthrough.

This self-justification is not convincing. The "results", the examples that he analyzes (prize-winners of open competitions, *haute couture*, certain types of surveys, etc.) are presented as expressions of the sociologist's "cheek" (to use Bourdieu's word); rather, they are often tedious and sometimes comical. For example, his remarks on "risotto", "paella", "rice curry" and "brown rice" seem like a parody; he informs us that to read even what seems to be the "most rigorous survey", one must analyze beforehand the social significance of the choices presented; one must see that "rice" obscures the fact that there are many kinds of rice, and they reflect different lifestyles. You have to reflect, he writes, on the taxonomies that, "coming straight out of the statisticians' unconscious social makeup, combine what should be kept separate (for example, green beans and kidney beans) and separate what could be combined (for example green beans and bananas, the latter being to fruit what the first are to vegetables)".[33] [There, we really should stop to reflect. First, he warns us that it is extremely difficult to interpret a survey — you need to be an expert; then, you need to be wary of the unconscious *social makeup* of the statisticians. We should take our hats off to sociologist Bourdieu's scientific approach. And, to conclude, I acknowledge that one fact had escaped me: that it might not be relevant to differentiate between green beans and bananas. . . Perhaps you are thinking, what meticulousness, what intuition, what cheek that Pierre Bourdieu has . . .]

Bourdieu's observations on workmen's purchases of socks, pajamas and bathrobes also appear parodic and of little interest. The bathrobe is "pretty much unknown in the rural and working class world"; it is "a typically middle-class attribute". In the same way, the sociologist teaches us that among women, "purchases of outerwear increase in number and value when one rises in the social hierarchy", and the same applies to men.[34] [A slow-minded reader might think that the opposite really would have been a discovery.] There, he touches on one of the very contestable and, in my eyes, somewhat enigmatic aspects of the sociologist: the belief that he has to be (really) scientific and intrepid while speaking about ridiculous, uninteresting or very well-known things. Who doesn't know, for example, that the bathrobe is "a typically middle-class attribute"? And what use is there in filling dozens of pages with details in this vein?

Relating that when Anatole France was child, he had dreamed of writing a French history "with all the details", Lucien Febvre said that in his own youth, the high school teachers seemed to recommend the same "puerile ideal". "It was said that, to them, history meant learning if not all the details, then at least as many details as possible, on Mr. de Charnacé's mission to the rivers of the North."[35] In the same way, Bourdieu wants to give us this plethora of details, but on secondary topics; and he doesn't bother to show how all these details relate to the major problems that he says he is explaining. How do all these details on beans, rice, sausages, chicken casserole, leg of lamb, socks, investments in cosmetics, kleenex and cloth handkerchiefs, etc.[36] lead him "to a reformulation of all the traditional questions on the beautiful, art, taste, culture"?

If you read and re-read Bourdieu's books, you find an avalanche of tedious conclusions, commentaries on things that are very well known or are of no interest (because of his *petitio principii*, his contention, — that everything has a meaning — to understand becomes to understand *every-*

thing), and commentaries on false or arbitrary results. There is no need to announce "an enormous work of empirical investigation and theoretical criticism" to bludgeon us with so many banalities, so many clichés cloaked in a "complex" language that in fact is so pretentious that it is very often amusing.

What is striking in Bourdieu's sociology is the contrast between the lack of boldness in many of his choices of objects (haute couture, a subject used for posing very broad problems? Is that a vital topic? Bourdieu repeats that (his) science touches on vital interests[37]) and the stentorian presentation of his results, his apparent "technicalness": ". . . only technical words allow us to say, and therefore to think, rigorously, about difficult things."[38] Does that mean that Lucien Febvre and Fernand Braudel, for example, did not think "rigorously" about their difficult objects?

The stress laid on "the laboratories of science" and "the manner", more than on results (it is his *modus operandi* which defines his "originality", Loïc J. D. Wacquant affirms[39]) are part of his will to impose his view, his fantasy vision of the world, his "opinions", as science. He wants to have us believe that he looks at things "up close", whereas he is "a grand theoretician", and a grand ideologue.[40]

Footnotes

1. "Le sociologue en question", in *Questions de sociologie,* Paris, Editions de Minuit, 1980, p. 39.
2. "Culture et politique", A talk given at the University of Grenoble, April 1980, in *Questions de sociologie, op. cit.,* p. 236.
3. *Prologue* to *Questions de sociologie, op. cit.,* p. 7.
4. "Le sociologue en question", *op. cit.,* p. 41.
5. *Ibid,* p. 38 and 39.
6. *Sur la télévision,* Paris, Liber/Raisons d'agir, 1997, pp. 88-89.
7. Pierre Bourdieu, "Le champ littéraire", *Actes de la recherche en sciences sociales,* No. 89, September 1991, p. 3.
8. "Bourdieu et Passeron sociologues de l'éducation", *Le Monde,* September 19, 1970, Suppl.
9. "Le sociologue en question", *op. cit.,* p. 38.
10. With Hans Haacke, *Libre-échange,* Paris, Seuil/Les Presses du réel, 1994, p. 110.
11. "Le sociologue en question", *op. cit.,* p. 49.
12. *Prologue* to *Questions de sociologie, op. cit.,* p. 7.
13. See: "Les trois états du capital culturel [Three states of cultural capital]", *Actes de la recherche en sciences sociales,* No. 30, November 1979, pp. 3-6. If Bourdieu would do any field work, he would avoid defining the incorporated, objectified, institutionalized state of cultural capital, for he would see that it is impossible to use such precise tools.
14. "Une science qui dérange", Interview with Pierre Thuillier, *La Recherche,* No. 112, June 1980, republished in *Questions de sociologie, op. cit.,* p. 28. [However, one should not forget what Bourdieu and Passeron had written ten years before: "While 'there is nothing to science but that which is hidden', we understand that sociology is partly associated with the historical forces which, in every era, force the truth of the relations of power to be revealed, even if only by forcing them to veil themselves still more." *La Reproduction,* Eléments pour une théorie du système d'enseignement, Paris, Editions de Minuit, 1970, p. 12].
15. "Le sociologue en question", *op. cit.,* p. 41.
16. "L'art de résister aux paroles", Interview with Didier Eribon, *Libération,* 3 and 4 November 1979, republished in *Questions*

de sociologie, op. cit., p. 14.
17. "Une science qui dérange", *op. cit.,* p. 20.
18. *La Distinction*, Critique sociale du jugement, Paris, Editions de Minuit, 1979, p. 596.
19. *Méditations pascaliennes,* Paris, le Seuil, 1997, p. 15.
20. *Prologue* to *Questions de sociologie, op. cit.,* p. 8.
21. "Le sociologue en question", *op. cit.,* p. 55.
22. "Comment libérer les intellectuels libres [How to free the free intellectuals?]" Interview with Didier Eribon, *Le Monde Sunday,* 4 May 1980, republished in *Questions de sociologie, op. cit.,* p. 67.
23. "Le sociologue en question", *op. cit.,* p. 56.
24. *Prologue. . . op. cit.,* p. 9.
25. "Le sociologue en question", *op. cit.,* p. 49.
26. "Ce que parler veut dire", speech before the congress of the AFEF, Limoges, October 30, 1977, appeared in *Le français aujourd'hui,* 41, March 1978, and suppl. to No 41, republished in *Questions de sociologie, op. cit.,* p. 95.
27. "Le sociologue en question", *op. cit.,* p. 44.
28. "Le paradoxe du sociologue", paper read at Arras (Noroit), October 1977, republished in *Questions de sociologie, op. cit.,* p. 93.
29. *Ibid.,* p. 94.
30. "Ce que parler veut dire", *op. cit.,* p. 105.
31. "Quelques propriétés des champs", a presentation given at the Advanced Teacher Training College, November 1976, in *Questions de sociologie, op. cit.,* p. 119.
32. "Le sociologue en question", *op. cit.,* p. 51.
33. Pierre Bourdieu, *La Distinction, op. cit.,* p. 20.
34. *Ibid,* pp. 224-225.
35. Lucien Febvre, "Vivre l'histoire" (1941), *Combats pour l'histoire,* Paris, Armand Colin, re-ed., 1992, p. 18.
36. To read Bourdieu, you have to keep reading the instructions on how to read Bourdieu. For example: "It is true that my analyses are the product of the application of very abstract concepts to very concrete things, such as statistics on the consumption of pyjamas, slips or trousers. Reading statistics on pyjamas while thinking of Kant, that does not come naturally . . . All our school training tends to prevent us from thinking of Kant in connection with pyjamas or to prevent us from thinking of pyjamas while reading Marx (I say Marx

instead of Kant, and you will let me get away with this all too easily, although, in this context, it is the same thing)." "Le sociologue en question", *op. cit.,* p. 40.

37. *Prologue. . . op. cit.,* p. 7.
38. "Ce que parler veut dire", *op. cit.,* p. 110.
    The sociologist who states that only technical words enable us to say, therefore to think about, difficult things, immediately gives a technical translation when he finds himself reporting words from the common "jargon", or rather slang. *Sur la télévision, op. cit.,* p. 25.
39. Loïc J. D. Wacquant, Presentation of: Pierre Bourdieu with Loïc J. D. Wacquant, *Réponses. Pour une anthropologie réflexive,* Paris, le Seuil, 1992, p. 7.
40. In *Réponses, op. cit.,* p. 88, Bourdieu describes the difficulty of his position in the sociological field. "In a way, I may appear close to the 'big theorists' (the structuralists, in particular) in that I insist on great structural balances, . . . ; on the other hand, I feel loyalty to those researchers who look at things close at hand . . . but I cannot accept the philosophy of the social world which is often at the basis of their interest in the details of the social practice and which is, to them at any rate, imposed by the nearer vision, and the theoretical 'myopia' that it encourages."

Chapter II

CONTRA INDICATIONS: "UNDERSTANDING", SAYS PIERRE BOURDIEU

I was a little late in reading "Understanding", 23 pages that Pierre Bourdieu published at the end of *The Weight of the World*,[1] for, I must admit, the book fell out of my hands long before page 903. In these final pages, Bourdieu sets out "the intentions and the principles of the procedures" that he and his (large) team applied in the research whose results are exposed in the preceding pages. In other words, he wants to teach us how to conduct an interview, which, according to him, "can be regarded as a form of *spiritual exercise*" (p. 912). These words made me want to stop reading. But I began again. I had to go on, and tell Bourdieu that he gives the same impression as a cyclist pedaling, and pedaling forever: he does not know when to put his foot on the ground.

> That image came to me while reading *Souvenirs de Pologne*, by Gombrowicz. Talking about a bicycle trip during which he and his companions had fueled themselves with wine and fruit, he recalls that he was so drunk that, when they arrived at their destination, he absolutely could not remember "how one gets off a bicycle". Pierre Bourdieu's work is striking in its pounding and ponderous repetitions, and his inability to get outside of himself, his theory. Putting a foot on the ground would mean coming out of himself, discussing, and not telling everyone else what they ought to be doing; it would mean reading other people's work, not making a fetish of a theory, not "applying" it imperturbably but testing it, adjusting it, and if need be, abandoning it.

Without taking up more time on that point, I'll just add that his language is deadly (or inspires laughter): bombast, posing, heaviness, playing on words in order to state the obvious (like "transcribing means writing, in the sense of re-writing" (p. 921), or "how can we do justice to his reasoning, without going along with his reasoning, without agreeing with his reasoning?" (p. 922). This tone is wearisome, as is Bourdieu's convocation of great authors — Spinoza and Aristotle — to talk about our daily work. But much graver are his pre-existing assumptions that he hammers on as scientific truths.

There is dissymmetry in the interview: true. But he adds social dissymmetry and cultural dissymmetry. The dissymmetry that has to do with the fact that it is the researcher who "starts the game and institutes the rule of the game" is reinforced by social dissymmetry, "whenever the researcher occupies a superior position than the survey respondent in the hierarchy of the various species of capital, and cultural capital in particular" (p. 905). He explains to us very learnedly what must be done "to surmount the obstacles tied to the differences in (social) conditions and, in particular, the fear of class-based contempt which, when the sociologist is perceived as socially superior, often adds to the very general, if not universal, fear of objectification" (p. 909). Is it the capital of "all kinds, and especially linguistic", with which Bourdieu shows himself richly and conspicuously endowed, that brings all those who are deprived of such capital to fear his capital, and thus to fear the differences between their conditions? "To control" (a word that he repeats endlessly), to reduce "the (inevitable) distortions" and "(inevitable) effects" ("without pretending to annul them", p. 906), to master, control, suspend, and limit the symbolic violence. . . , Bourdieu "teaches" us two of the principal conditions of a nonviolent communication: social proximity and familiarity.

Bourdieu's discourse on dissymmetry is unreal; it is a projection of his vulnerabilities, his anguishes and his dreams that he transfers onto the world. The dominated as he depicts them are women and men who are mentally prostrate before the "legitimate order" which supposedly has the ability to impose the dominant values on everyone, making them accept them, making them internalize them. That is why they are afraid of the sociologist, who is "perceived as socially superior" (p. 909). To "see" the "dominated" in this light, you have to have really kept yourself far away from the real world.[2]

In his *Pascalian Meditations* (1997), Bourdieu assures us that he never "shied away" from "what are considered the humblest tasks in the trade of ethnologist or sociologist: direct observation, interviews, coding of data and statistical analysis"; these (humble) activities "were one of the opportunities that allowed me to escape being cooped up in the scholastic world of offices, libraries, courses and discourse. . ."[3] However, when he is telling us how to go about the practice of giving interviews, he shows that he is a man of "courses and discourse" and not man of practical experience. His lessons rest on an invented view of the dominated and on a very limited number of interviews, and they are diametrically opposed to accepted interview practices; people who regularly conduct interviews have criticized his method, in detail.[4]

By way of contrast, I don't mind presenting a survey that I conducted among French citizens from Algeria. In 1996 and 1997, I questioned 135 of them, from all the trades: mechanics, professors of medicine, cleaning ladies, lawyers, hairdresser's assistants, homemakers, farmers ("large" and small), craftsmen, fishermen, teachers, dressmakers, commercial salesmen, etc.. It never crossed my mind to detail all the background of this work in progress and to lecture on how it should be done — but it is, indeed, necessary to respond with concrete, precise examples to Bourdieu's general pronouncements. Perhaps it is because I am not endowed with too much linguistic capital, and capital of all kinds, that nobody expressed anything with regard to the "social distance" that separated us (in such a research project, conducted among so varied a population, it is clear that this distance must come into play in every sense); and no one was afraid of a potential (or latent?) "class-based contempt". How, then, does Bourdieu conduct his "spiritual exercise" so that his interlocutors feel inferior, dominated, or fearful?

For he takes such great pains, he goes through so many contortions to limit, reduce, thwart, etc., the distortions "registered in the very structure of the survey relationship" (p. 904). I had no familiarity with the Algerian French whom I was going to question. I did not know them and they were very distant from me, since they had been born, had grown up, and had worked in a different society that I had never known nor even seen. Not feeling attacked, threatened, dominated, nor forced (symbolically), my interlocutors spoke at length; they laughed, and sometimes cried; very often, we had a glass of wine before or after the interview; sometimes we had lunch; often, they went back with me in the car. I understood very well the meaning of the gestures of these exiles — who usually feel ostracized and this time, felt recognized — without experiencing any need to explain it (or the theory). I repeat: I had no familiarity with this population; and with a population so diversified socially, what can I say about the social distance between interviewer and interviewee?

Pierre Bourdieu, recognizing that "the universe of social categories that can be reached under optimal conditions for familiarity has its limits", extends this universe by referring to the strategy that William Labov used in his study of black speech in Harlem. To neutralize "the effect of imposing the legitimate language", Labov had the survey conducted by young Blacks. In the same way, explains Bourdieu, "We tried, whenever possible, to neutralize one of the major factors of distortion in the survey relationship by giving training in survey techniques to people who could access, on the basis of familiarity, the categories of interviewees that we wished to reach" (p. 908). Having to resort to this strategy would certainly put a limit on the fields of investigation for a solitary researcher!

> When I am conducting a survey it often happens that I have to question people who speak: with all kinds of accent (a strong Polynesian or Sicilian accent, for example), with faulty syntax (an abundance of Hispanic expressions, extremely simplified grammatical constructions, etc.), sometimes with coarse vocabulary, sometimes with several words of *patois*; in the beginning, those escaped me, but I picked them up very quickly. Most of the time, people talk (to me) the way they normally talk: no fear or inhibition before "the effect of imposition of the legitimate language". I simply try to be clear, to speak with "ordinary" words. In his interview with Ali and François, "two young people from the North of France" (pp. 87-99), Pierre Bourdieu lists the words: shit, shit's creek, dip shit, ass, asshole, hell, hell hole, fuck, fucking shit, fuck off, fuck it all, schmuck, dick, dickhead. . . , sometimes picking up a word that has come up in conversation but in other cases, introducing it. He is sure that, by demonstrating his "familiarity", he is "neutralizing" (as much as possible) the effect of imposing the legitimate language; in fact, he is exhibiting a false familiarity and a genuinely anachronistic paternalism. Bourdieu cannot "prove" why, "scientifically", the interviewer-sociologist *must* be coarse when questioning members of the popular classes.

Bourdieu notes that nothing is easier than "imposing problems" (p. 918). You may have noticed that in giving us lessons, Bourdieu is mostly correcting us: against the "pure *laissez-faire*" of the non-directive interview, (p. 906), against rushed interviews or interviews on the fly, chance encounters, pollsters who lack specific competence. . . (p. 911.) [It is tempting to agree with him, but whom is he talking about?] However, if there is any lesson that we should give him (!), it is that he has conducted a bad interview here, for he directs it heavily, he guides it and even corrects it.

The purpose of what he calls "*caused and accompanied self-analysis*" is, through "questions and suggestions", to make the survey respondent produce the explanation of what he is: "to bring to light the social determinants of his opinions and his practices" (p. 913), "to construct their own point of view on themselves and the world and. . . to make manifest the point, within this world, from which they see themselves and see the world" (p. 915). The explanation produced must conform to that which the investigator knows in advance, thanks to his "immense knowledge". "It is only when research is based on a prior knowledge of realities that it can bring forth the realities that it intends to record" (p. 916). One would like to know, then, what Bourdieu "learns" during an interview, in addition to "*the felicity of expression*", "the extraordinary *expressive intensity*" of the statement of "long-reserved or repressed reflections" (p. 915).

In a survey, as in all human relations, there are distances: they are different from the social distance that is Bourdieu's central theory, that gives it structure. There are fertile distances: I am a woman and I have mostly questioned men, Mediterranean men; the majority of them coming from the rim of the Mediterranean basin, they live in a society with Mediterranean morals. Bourdieu has nothing to say about this completely essential characteristic, sex (the "distortions" and "the effects" that it produces. . .); he knows only (social) classes and classifications.[5] He speaks about "sympathy between women" "to partially overcome the social distance" ("the existence of various bonds of secondary solidarity likely to give an indisputable guarantee of sympathetic comprehension", p. 909) and he dodges the major problem of the relation of the sexes in the conduct of a survey. He sees "sympathy" between women only as a "secondary solidarity". . . ; how does he see the relationship in a private woman-man conversation in a interview?

Another source of distance is age. Many of my interviewees were over 75 years old. This distance facilitates certain confidences; it obliges the investigator to be more attentive and inclines the elderly to display a kind of "abandon". Here, the gender difference reinforces the (positive) effects of the age distance: a long history of fieldwork proves this, in the results gathered.

And trade is another form of distance. My overt trade — historian — encourages the curiosity of those with degrees (i.e., those who are endowed with capital, etc.) and the sympathy of those who have none; that does not at all mean — really, not at all — that, as Bourdieu believes, that they feel inferior, or that they are afraid of what they will say, or that they make an effort to give a good impression, etc.. They receive the researcher as somebody who has written books, and who will write another, on them. This forthcoming book pleases them and gives them a kind of confidence; of course, when it comes time to leave, they often ask if it was interesting for us, if it was what we were looking for (and their tone indicates that they very much hope so), if they are going to appear in the book, etc..

That does not express either fear or inferiority; nor excessive respect for the investigator (endowed with capital, etc.), nor humility, embarrassment, nor shame. Which is fortunate, for if the "intrusion" (which is "always a little bit arbitrary", p. 905) of the sociologist or the historian might cause the interviewee a sense of an inadequacy, a sense of inferiority, then the surveys would have to be stopped. . . Therefore the distances that I encounter — sex, age, occupation — seem positive, to me, and they are easy to evaluate: I have to be at my most attentive when it comes to the (very) elderly; the gender difference contributes to certain surprises; and other people's occupations, often so different from mine that I have difficulty to imagine them (a surgeon, like a home-based dressmaker or a fisherman), leads me to want to go further. There was never complicity from the outset (except for my keen interest and their desire "to be acknowledged") and, certainly, during the interview, there is more tension toward the surveyed, more attention, and more respect accorded to the "alien" than to the "familiar".

Bourdieu defines the conditions necessary to the interview very distinctly. "The investigator has no chance of really being up to his task unless he has immense knowledge in this area, acquired sometimes throughout a lifetime of research and also, more directly, through previous interviews with this respondent or with advisors" (p. 911). Let us look back: a few pages earlier, Bourdieu was talking about all the advantages of familiarity, a physicist questioning a physicist, an unemployed person surveying another unemployed person, an actor, an actor, each one sharing with the other "nearly all the characteristics that can serve as major explanatory factors of his practices and his representations" (p. 908). One wonders, then, how he would have been able to acquire "immense knowledge" in taking surveys. No need to worry about that, for Bourdieu admits that the part-time researchers that he had trained in technical investigation (p. 908) came back with surveys that could not be published. "They delivered hardly anything more than socio-linguistic data unable to provide the instruments of their own interpretation" (p. 909). Bourdieu discovered that one of the major reasons of these failures resides in "the perfect agreement" between the surveyor and the surveyee, so much so that the surveyee omits stating what "goes without saying" (p. 909). It took him a huge amount of time to discover something so obvious! However, he had told us — you remember — that social proximity and familiarity ensure "two of the principal conditions of a 'nonviolent communication'" (p. 907). Aren't there some contradictions in Bourdieu's lessons?

In short, against what Bourdieu says (his reflections "on the relation of communication in its general form" waver between obvious facts and certitudes that are shockingly imprecise), I have weighed what the researcher knows, through his trade, his "professionalism", and his seniority in practice, his assets and his limitations. We don't need a professor to point out to us "the distortions" and "the effects" of the interview process: it is a fact of our daily life. We know very well that the interviewee expects us to listen — and I listen, without ever having to "haul myself out of the drowsiness and inattention fostered by the illusion of having already seen this and heard this before" (p. 912).

Every meeting is unique; we know that from birth! But Bourdieu's sociology has spent its time surfing over the individualities, and after ignoring them, this is where it has ended up; that is why he goes in circles, why he measures everything against a Procrustean bed. Therefore I listen; and I question, going back to what has already been said or touched upon, and which interests me or surprises me; I try to further go and, at the same time, obviously, never to force; that is a fundamental attitude. The interviewees — women, men, rich or poor, from the left or the right, well-endowed or stripped of all species of capital, etc. — expect one to listen to them with sympathy. And very often, the interviewer, deeply interested, is: impassioned, shocked, moved, impressed, but also sometimes pained or revolted or made indignant — *sub rosa*, in these last cases — by the Others' stories. Sometimes, of course, the interview fails: generally because the person, quite simply, appeared antipathetic to the researcher, because of a personality trait, and not because of his "opinions" or his "inferiority", or his appearance.[6] In every project we thus make "mistakes", and we see them very clearly. For we do not practice without reflecting. After every action, we critique our work, and we establish provisional assessments, but this activity is discreet. This constant reflection on one's practical work has no claim to any status on its own, to any higher status.

Afterwards comes all the work of transcription, analysis, etc., in short, the pursuit of the trade. But we have chosen this work, and we go about it serenely. There is no need to comment on it with ponderous and priggish pedantry, to puff it up, to present it as if it were hard to do. Bourdieu writes as if he were practicing a very difficult craft, a perilous exercise: "To say that the interview is a spiritual exercise, that cost me. . . I have always thought that, always felt that. . . I had to reach my current age, and I had to have a little more chutzpah, to be able to commit that transgression."[7] Finally, at his age, he can arrive at "a kind of intellectual love" (p. 914). But after such trials! Such painful, arid spiritual exercises, before attaining "an outlook that consents to necessity, like 'God's intellectual love', i.e. the natural order, which Spinoza held to be the supreme form of knowledge" (p. 914).

In his unpleasant language, Bourdieu gives the idea that his is an unpleasant profession, in a world that is itself unpleasant and even more than hard: painful, cruel, an existence rent by hierarchies, distances, symbolic violence, etc. etc.. This is no longer the weight of the world, but of the despair of the world. And the woe of the researcher.

Looking at the late 20th century with the eye of a 19th century ideologue, or someone from the *proletarian Left*, Bourdieu reveals a desperate vision of a motionless world, or perhaps one that is going from bad to worse[8]. . . If the world were such as he describes, why would he be investing himself in so many "interventions" and "transgressions", so many appeals to a countervailing power? If the world were only that, how could we live? Thank God, the world is far more alive, far more complex, more exciting, more "free"; it is more variegated than the one that Bourdieu's sociology fabricates.

And so, we will have to leave aside his lessons, and leave him to absorb himself in his "reasons to act", his "transgressions" and his "subversions". We'll pass over his paroxysms and pause, in order to have a good laugh, on the observation made in the preface of *Free Exchange* (1994): "One cannot fail to notice that one (Bourdieu) and the other (Hans Haacke) take advantage of their social consecration . . . to go on making transgressions. . . " In other words: when you are no longer under any risk, you can take some — for example, by saying whatever you like. . .

Footnotes

1. Pierre Bourdieu (under the direction of), *La Misère du monde,* Paris, le Seuil, 1993.
2. The historian Philippe Joutard made some pertinent remarks on the interview in 1983 in: *Ces voix qui nous viennent du passé*, Paris, Hachette,1983, Chapters 7 and 8. Look at what he has to say, in particular, about the "false-problem" of "the inequality of relations which is born from the different sociocultural statuses or the position of the questioner." "During the conversation, the inequality is not located in the usual place." "Does the problem really occur in terms of dominate-dominated? I never had that feeling" (p. 201).
3. Pierre Bourdieu, *Méditations pascaliennes,* Paris, le Seuil, 1997, p. 13.
4. Cf. Nonna Mayer, "L'entretien selon Pierre Bourdieu", *Revue française de sociologie,* XXXVI, 1995, pp. 355-370; Gerard Grumberg and Etienne Schweisguth, "Bourdieu et la misère : une approche réductionniste", *Revue française de science politique,* vol. 46, No 1, 1996, pp. 134-155.
5. Didn't Bourdieu affirm, in *Distinction,* Paris, Editions de Minuit, 1979, p. 119: "The properties of sex are as indissociably properties of class as the yellow of a lemon is inseparable from its acidity: a class is defined by its most essential rules as to the place and the value that it grants the two sexes and to their socially constituted provisions. That is why there are as many manners of expressing femininity as there are classes and fractions of class. . ."

   "Male Domination", which he analyzes somewhat belatedly (*Actes de la recherche en sciences sociales,* No 84, September 1990, pp. 4-31) does not lead him to change his views on the practice of the interview; however, gender is an essential dimension. His views on women's conduct are so outdated! "Self-subordination, which is accompanied by a certain anxiety, as testified by the glances which the docile wives would throw at their husbands and the investigator throughout the entire exchange" (p. 13). That is an old stereotype, it is not the real world.
6. Something to ponder: "How. . . can we evoke, without stir-

ring up class racism, the hairstyle of a minor employee and how can we communicate, without ratifying it, the impression that it inevitably produces on the eye that has been trained by the canons of legitimate esthetics. . . ?" (p. 922). It would be useful to inquire, today, into whether legitimate esthetics exists; that would prevent any confusion between "the belief" in legitimacy and (indisputable) legitimacy. Of course, the eye of the sociologist who speaks here, who is "subversive" and militant, cannot have been trained by "the canons of legitimate esthetics".

7. Pierre Bourdieu, *Avant-propos dialogué* with: Jacques Master, *L'autobiographie d'un paranoïaque,* Paris, Anthropos, 1994, p. XVIII.
8. Bourdieu had just published in *Contre-feux* (Paris, Liber-Raisons d'agir, 1998) a small text entitled: "Le néo-libéralisme, utopie (en voie de réalisation) d'une exploitation sans limites [Neoliberalism, Utopia (in the process of realization) of unlimited exploitation]" (pp. 108-119). Were the proletarians less exploited in 1870 or 1900 than today — or tomorrow?

Chapter III

Odds and Ends —
The Social Critique of Taste
On *Distinction* (1979)

Pierre Bourdieu, who presented himself at that time as science itself, apparently thought that it was scientific to ridicule André Malraux in *Distinction, A Social Critique of the Judgment of Taste*. This is how he presented *The Voices of Silence*: it "wraps up in the bric-a-brac of Spenglerian metaphysics a culture of odds and ends, phlegmatically associating 'the most contradictory intuitions', hasty borrowings from Schlosser and Worringer, rhetorically exalted platitudes, purely incantatory litanies of exotic names, and insights that are called brilliant because they are not even false" (p. 379). I would not apply all these judgments to *Distinction*, but one phrase does seem appropriate: *odds and ends*.

This fat volume purports to be a social criticism of taste, which is inevitably also a portrayal of social classes and lifestyles; and it also purports to be the reformulation of "all the traditional questions on the beautiful, on art, taste, culture". The book claimed to be an absolutely new object: Bourdieu the iconoclast knew that his sociology of taste clashed with "one of the most vital questions in the battle that is waged on the field of the dominant class and the field of cultural production", that this ground was *quintessentially* that of "the denial of the social" (p. 9). This ambitious project generated an avalanche of statistics, tables and graphs, a torrent of commentary, a cameo appearance by Kant for his *A Critique of Judgment*, reams of photographs, excerpts from interviews, etc., in short, an enormous pile of odds and ends.

A few aspects of this sociology should have caught and should still hold the reader's attention, since they so clearly evidence its ideological nature. First of all, the inconsistencies, the biases, the weakness of the data upon which this research bases its conclusions; then, the objectification that the sociologist says he manages but which, through the tone he adopts, is transmuted into generalized contempt; and especially the pessimism, the anachronism of the image he gives of the popular classes.

Bourdieu makes plain his disgust for the tastes and the lifestyles of the popular classes. In fact, he has pretty much imagined these tastes and caricatured certain features. He has interpreted and, more important, he has generalized a few examples that he may, perhaps, have observed. His description is not realistic, it vacillates between a militant, demanding diatribe (Thorez or Auguste Lecœur? The proletarian Left? In any case, a dated, obsolete line of talk) and a fearful discourse, ignoring "ordinary" daily life, a line that, in the final analysis, is reactionary.

His analyses were based on a survey conducted in 1963 with a sample of 692 men and women in Paris, in Lille and in a small provincial town, and on a subsequent survey in 1967-1968, bringing the number of people questioned up to 1217. His reflections on method recognize the limitations of investigating such a topic by questionnaire; it is never more than "*makeshift*", he writes (underlined in his text, p. 591). The survey questionnaire (published pp. 599-604) contains all of Bourdieu's foregone conclusions and the distortions of judgment (of "tastes") that he imposed by employing heavily biased terms — negatively (for example, "Do you prefer to buy nice clothes," "smart, fancy, sharp", etc.), or positively (for him) — "or having your friends over for the evening", "a little party" — about which he will then talk with a faked sense of familiarity. He asked four questions about painting, two of which suggest judgments. Question 22 required each subject to choose the view that was closest to his own opinion: "I am not interested in painting", "Museums aren't my strong suit, I can't really appreciate them", "Painting is fine but it is hard to talk about, you have to be knowledgeable to discuss it", "I love the Impressionists", "I am interested in abstract painting as much as in the classical schools". Question 25 asked for an opinion on three statements, only three (and the sociologist was supposed to withhold the answer that he expected from the dominated): "Modern painting is mindless scribbling, a child could do it" or, "I don't care who painted it, or how he did it" or, "I cannot appreciate painting, because I do not see myself in it".

The quality of the questionnaire casts doubt on the quality of the results. Similarly, the list of musical works that he suggests, and the judgments on "classical music", are shocking in every way.[1] The questionnaire is hardly scientific, because the topics selected are very restricted, very biased, and sometimes too vague to be interpretable.[2] As for the "Observation Schedules" recorded by the surveyor, and no doubt established by the lead sociologist, on many points they show great ignorance (about ways of dressing, lifestyles) and on almost every point, contempt and contestable ulterior motives. "Note whether the accent is 'strong, slight, or none'".[3] [Can we be sure that all the surveyors had a good ear, and a good accent? For Bourdieu, the "strong" accent" is indicative of the popular classes. But how many dominant, and dominant-dominated (including among the professors at the University of Paris or the College of France) have an accent! What is Bourdieu going to make of that?]

"The enormous empirical labor" (of which Bourdieu boasts) is the "mobilization", around the investigation, of a mass of statistical data reflecting the economic culture, consumption of food and clothing, theater habits, preferences in the areas of education, sexuality, sports, etc.. These data were not at all scientific, for they had been collected in response to questions from, for example, a magazine (*Marie-Claire*), the French broadcasting company, a government Ministry, etc.. Bourdieu is tireless in his minute commentaries on the subdivisions within the lower middle class (the declining petty bourgeoisie, the executant petty bourgeoisie and the new petty bourgeoisie) and on the subdivisions of taste within these segments; how could he now use these complementary, heterogeneous, none too scientific, approximate, in short, not very reliable data sources?

These surveys relied, moreover, on relatively "limited samples" (p. 610) and they generally used a system of grading that lumped together all the professions into five categories: 1) farmers; 2) laborers; 3) owners of industry and businesses; 4) junior executives, commercial employees, office workers, support staff; 5) managerial staff and liberal professions. Therefore, Bourdieu can only have found statistics that were largely unrefined. How sure can he be, then, of what he says about the tastes of the declining category, and about the different tastes of the new petty bourgeoisie? In the first category, he puts skilled laborers and small tradesmen; he says that the second group is "emerging" in professions of presentation and representation — occupations related to medical and social services (vocational counseling, marriage counseling, youth leaders), arts management and production (fashion, interior design, advertising, marketing, sales) etc., and also in already established professions (nurses, craftsmen and artisans); and within the occupation of artisan "in the old sense" — tapestry makers, upholsterers, ironworkers, cabinetmakers, picture framers, goldsmiths, jewelers, gilders and engravers — in the last ten years or so have cropped up a new generation of jewelry-makers, silk screeners, ceramicists, and weavers (whew!), who "are linked, by their lifestyle, to the cultural intermediaries" (p. 415). Where does he find all the data that enables him to discuss the heterogeneity of the trajectories of the new petty bourgeoisie, of the duality of social origins and all the correlations he draws? And so on. There is no linkage between the quantified results of the surveys and his detailed comments. How can he have precise information on the tastes of the (declining) tradesmen and on those of ironworkers or manufacturers of hand-printed fabrics (of the new petty bourgeoisie)?

Bourdieu's analyses of the petty bourgeoisie are, of course, called scientific; he claims that the objectifying reduction that he performs has nothing in common with "the contempt of class" that crops up in so many writings on the petty bourgeoisie ("think of Marx talking about Proudhon", p. 390); for his reduction "relates the properties of the *habitus*. . . to the objective conditions of which they are the product" (p. 390). Having given this warning once again, he is free to reel off the most shopworn clichés about the petty bourgeoisie. "They stick together in a tight-knit but narrow and somewhat oppressive family. It is not by chance that the adjective "petty", or its synonyms, always more or less pejorative, can be paired with everything about the petty bourgeois, everything he says, thinks, does, has or is, even to his morals, albeit his strong suit: strict and rigorous, there is something narrow and constrained about him, tense and nervous, insular and rigid because he is formalistic and scrupulous. Petty concerns, petty needs — the petty bourgeois is a bourgeois who lives stingily" (p. 390).

One almost wants to continue with: "The petty security that his petty economies afford the petty worker, living his petty little life in his petty little house. . . ", etc.. The author of these last remarks, an honors graduate of the ENS Teachers' College, who was a regular columnist pumping out articles in this vein, after World War I, knew that he was not making science but rather politics. The ENS had taught him sophistication; week in and week out, he wrote with a great facility about the platitudes of his day, of his milieu, handily stringing together oxymorons and giving the impression that there was some underlying analysis. This is by the very prolix Pierre Gaxotte ("La hideuse mesure", *Je suis partout*, August 1, 1936).

> During a recent research project, it was useful that I had read hundreds of articles by Pierre Gaxotte, published between the two wars; they helped me to reflect on the teachings of the ENS, of which this very abundant prose, always peremptory and often vacuous, is a product. This training teaches students to take bluffing for audacity, and writing for "work", whereas it actually functions as a game, and as a word game, as the elaboration of ideas. That is why I do not see that Pierre Bourdieu has "betrayed" the ENS, as he claims.

The great bulk of what Bourdieu writes about the petty bourgeoisie strongly resembles what certain "bourgeois" — in fact, the "petty intellectuals" — say about the petty bourgeoisie. And he must know that, since he repeatedly claims that what he says has nothing to do with the "mannered prophecies" or "political anathema" of which the bourgeois are the mouthpieces, even if we think we see a resemblance. "Those who can offer less cantankerous virtues and show a less 'ungrateful' face forget that the characteristics they condemn are the inevitable counterpart of the mechanisms that ensure that individuals can move up, i.e. the advancement of suitable individuals, and they make as if the 'vices' and 'virtues' of the petty bourgeoisie (who — shall I say it? — can only be defined as such in relation to the dominant ethic) and only those of the petty bourgeoisie, were due to the individual and not to structures, under the pretext that the structures left them free to 'choose' their alienation" (p. 390).

This lesson having been hammered home, one wonders why Bourdieu describes to us so lengthily, so repetitively, the "pure and empty" cultural goodwill of the petty bourgeoisie (p. 406), the repressive rigor of the declining segments, the ascetic rigor of the emerging fractions, or the petty bourgeoisie's avid claim to upward mobility, etc., etc.; for his "theory" has already given us the conclusion, has told us how to understand what we see every day: that people on the way up, for example, can only be what they are.

While the mocking tone that the "objectifying sociologist" uses in speaking about "those who, making a profession out of proselytism, have ended up making proselytism a profession" (social work, continuing education, arts management, counseling in pedagogy or sexuality) (p. 428) may be aggravating, his representation of the popular classes is more shocking. The chapter on "The Choice of the Necessary", on the taste of the most popular classes, makes up only 28 pages, whereas the preceding chapter, on the petty bourgeoisie, "Cultural Goodwill", is more than double that: 67 pages.[4] Bourdieu apparently must have felt less at ease talking about the popular classes; what he calls objectification (and which is an assertion of his superiority) probably seemed fraught with consequences and politically assailable. What he suggests there is stated without proof: thus he associates the position of the dominated with a feeling of humiliation, of shame. Claiming that a feeling of shame is part of the condition of the "dominated" shows great ignorance of the real world and the "compromise" of Life.

Bourdieu, always criticizing future criticisms, invents them. In reference to *Distinction*, he affirms that his discourse aims to be declarative, and that readers see it as performative. "Describing the working class as it is makes me look as though I want lock it into what it is, as a destiny, as though I want to put it down, or set it on a pedestal."[5] But what he is criticized for is not that he exalts or denigrates the working class, but for not describing it as it is; he paints a picture that brings to mind cheap 19th century novels.

In his chapter on the tastes of the popular classes, two aspects alternate: unproven and *unprovable* generalities (like the one that we have just criticized and rejected), and an accumulation, sometimes an effusion, of statistics aiming to prove propositions that are generally of *limited scope.*

> For example: "The members of the popular classes 'have no idea' of what might be the privileged classes' system of needs nor have they any more notion of their resources, something about which they have a very abstract knowledge that bears no correspondence with reality" (p. 437). And he reels off the workers' responses (and also those of the executives, industrialists and members of the liberal professions, and rank and file employees) to the question: What is the price of a good meal in central Paris? Once more, we are saturated with statistics that contribute little: for example, 13% of the workers say they don't know (as against 2% of the executives), 13% of the workers say "over 50 francs", and 14% of the executives say the same thing, etc.. To go over such minor facts at such length, fifty times, is pretty close to useless.

Various series of figures are presented in a tone of scholarly knowledge, dissecting the variations in breakfast choices between "salted, substantial foods" (meat, cheese) and foods that are "soft and sweet" (honey, jam) according to professional categories (p. 445); and the results are neither new, nor unexpected, nor "disturbing". When it comes to the variations in use of make-up and beauty care, the numbers are followed by personal comments that are seldom exact and that are, in certain cases, deprecatory and shocking in what they imply. Thus the women of the popular classes, he states, do not allow themselves the attentions, the care, that would enable the body "to ensure or preserve its health, slenderness, beauty". He adds a comment of a dark misanthropy: because "they *do not have enough self-esteem*" (italicized in the text, p. 443). This proposition *cannot be proven*; how would one even go about establishing such an assertion?

Many of Bourdieu's comments have no more basis than this statement; he writes what he thinks, and he wants to make us believe that he is only translating scientific results. Just as he declares that the women of the popular classes "do not have enough self-esteem", he thinks that members of the popular classes make it "a point of honor to contradict the image that the dominant ones hold of their class". He talks about an intention of "rehabilitation" (p. 440). [On topics like this, one notes that Bourdieu confuses *one* specific militant approach with the expression of *the* popular truth].

He can make this statement only because he has suggested the idea that the dominated could be, would be, ashamed of themselves. The "dominated", according to him, accept the domination in a certain sense. "It would be easy to enumerate the features of the lifestyles of the dominated classes that, through feelings of incompetence, failure or cultural unworthiness, lock them into a form of recognition of the dominant values" (p. 448). What is the basis for this assertion that they have a feeling of incompetence, of failure, of cultural unworthiness? What a long, difficult, subtle — in fact, impossible — job it would be to conduct the research necessary to formulate such a judgment!

Many of his comments ring false; Bourdieu abuses slang expressions like "à la bonne franquette" and "bon vivant", which he proposed in his questionnaire, and words that smack of a higher or lower degree of sophistication, as if quotation marks (which he uses in a very calculated way), certified that these are typically popular words; in fact, Bourdieu uses the words that he attributes to them himself.

In order to "show" the "effects of domination", Bourdieu lines up the obvious ("As much as by the absence of all consumption of luxury products, imported liquor or paintings, champagne or concerts, cruises or art exhibitions, caviar or antiques. . . ", p. 448 — was it necessary to emphasize at such length that there is an "absence of consumption of luxury" in the popular classes?) along with remarks written in a way that betrays a certain contempt; he speaks, for example, of "*downward substitutes*" (could there be substitutes upwards? Did he have to put this expression in italics?). In this specific case, the comment that follows is militant: these substitutes are an "indication of dispossession to the second power that accepts the imposition of a definition of the goods worth having" (p. 450). However, as mentioned above, Bourdieu revealed that the popular classes "'have no idea' of what might be needs of the privileged classes nor of their resources"; they ape something about which they have no idea. . .

The commentaries are often inflated by the "conceptual" tone he adopts, and this tone captures one's attention even more since the writing is dissonant. For example, the reader must be able to follow his switches from the register of "the *in chiasmus* structure of the dominant class" (p. 130) to the register of "the big-bellied business owner" (p. 358). Everywhere, the lofty tones of the ENS are enlivened by boyish impudence. The commentaries are blown out of proportion in relation to their basis, as well — one has the impression that the sociologist elevates the tone in order to compensate for the fact that he never attains his goal, expressing a certain distress through this greed to accumulate bits and pieces of "proof".

Often, an avalanche of statistics is given in support of a statement that may well be interesting but that could have been said, and clearly understood, without making it look like a proposition that was difficult to express and to render comprehensible. A paragraph of eighteen lines announces a rather simple point that is further illustrated by a pile of statistics: foremen, who have a much higher income than that of skilled workmen, eat the same things as they do (starchy food, pork, potatoes, poultry) for they "remain attached to the popular values of 'eating well'"; but they consume them in greater quantity. Consumption of "*costly*" items, "that the workmen must limit" (fine sausages, wines, coffee, sugar, butter) goes up sharply with the foremen. A great part of their budget goes to food (almost the same percentage as among the skilled workmen) and the overall sum they spend in this category is equal to that of managerial staff; however, they do not share their consumption of "expensive" items, which are "characteristic of the bourgeois lifestyle" (veal, lamb, fish, shellfish, citrus fruits, etc.). Bourdieu then explains that when managerial workers' income levels change, the logic driving their changing food purchases *is not same logic as that of the workmen. . .* (pp. 437-438).

Many discoveries are on this level; I will not go as far as to say, like Groucho Marx, that any four-year-old knows that, but in fact such well-known things do not elicit any resistance from readers and do not represent any daring campaign by the sociologist. All of what I have just summarized is detailed at length by Bourdieu to show the whole range of a proposition that he had just developed and that affirmed "the net effect of the *habitus*". This paragraph deserves to be reproduced, and deserves to be read carefully:

> "What the statistics record in the form of *systems of needs* is nothing but the coherence of the choices of a *habitus*. And the inability 'to spend more' or differently, i.e. to reach the system of needs implied by a higher level of resources, is the best attestation of the impossibility of reducing the propensity to consume to the capacities of appropriation or the *habitus* to the economic conditions strictly defined (for example, as they can be apprehended in terms of a given income level). While everything leads us to believe there is a direct correspondence between income level and consumption, in fact it is because taste is almost always the product of economic conditions identical to those in which it functions, so that one can impute to income a causal relationship that it exerts only in *association* with the *habitus* that it produced. In fact, the *effectiveness of the habitus* is seen clearly when the same incomes are associated with very different patterns of consumption, which can be understood only if one supposes the intervention of different principles of selection" (p. 437).

If I were teaching, I would assign a text like that to my students to be boiled down to five or six lines; isn't concision a quality of clear thought?

It seems to me that he has drawn sufficient attention to the weakness of his empirical data and the duality of the comments (and of well-known facts, or imagined and unprovable propositions) to draw this recitation of examples to a close. The book is annoying in its prolixity of commentary on the most prosaic subjects. I read again and again the interminable page about eating with the front of the teeth (who does that? what do they eat that way?) and wiping one's nose with a big cloth handkerchief (p. 211). The objectifying and reflexive sociologist seems to be enchanted by writing about "unimportant" things. But why do it? To reveal and explain what?

Having set out to conduct a very interesting and difficult project — which Bourdieu transforms in his remarks into a vital, lofty and perilous project — we arrive at an end product that forces us to navigate through a sea of statistics, on subjects that often are of little interest, and prolix, turgid comments that "make one's attention ache".[6] Under this bombast lies a way of thinking that is vicious rather than rebellious. The author is opposed, for eternity.

Distinction tries to get us to believe that it is a scientific work. And perhaps its postscript, "*Elements for a 'vulgar' critique of pure critiques*", a critique of Kant's *A Critique of Judgment* (pp. 565-585) (ah! Take a look at "Parerga and paralipomena", pp. 578-583) does contribute to giving this bric-a-brac some status as an "erudite work". You can read it every which way, in vain; you can struggle to wade through so many insignificant details, elaborated and annotated; you will not find, there, the promised reformulation of "all the traditional questions on the beautiful, on art, taste, culture". And that is why I have not addressed, here, anything of the beautiful, of art, or culture.

Footnotes

1. I have to wonder how Bourdieu came up with the five choices he offers:
   – classical music is complicated;
   – classical music is not for us;
   – I like classical music but I do not know much about it;
   – I like classical music, for example the Strauss waltzes;
   – any good quality music interests me.
   The survey respondents had to choose which judgment is nearest to their own opinion.
2. In designating the "kinds" of books, Bourdieu proposes, for example, historical narratives, political works. If he starts from such broad categories, how can he claim to make a precise and unquestionable analysis?
3. If Bourdieu had any practical experience, he would have not drawn up so false, and therefore unreal, a plan of observation, from which nothing "serious" can be derived; this plan reflects outdated stereotypes and expresses a certain contempt of class which, in our day, has become rare. Read page 605, to evaluate how scientific his comments are.
4. In this third part on the "Class tastes and life styles", the dominant class requires even more pages than the petty-bourgeoisie: "The meaning of the distinction", pp. 293-364. This indefinite and indefinable class is divided into many varying categories: business owners in industry and trade, sometimes together, sometimes separate, professors and higher education teachers, members of the liberal professions (themselves divided into two sub-groups, "particularly separated in terms of cultural capital"). Later (p. 305), we find "the intellectuals, both certified and apprentices" who are not defined; sometimes Bourdieu speaks about the cultural practices "of educators and intellectuals", "the ascetic aristocratism" of professors and public sector executives (p. 325) as opposed to the "taste for luxury" of the members of the liberal professions; "the old business bourgeoisie" crops up, along with the new bourgeoisie (p. 353), private sector executives, as distinct from the captains of industry and trade; and there is information on the financial directors of major companies (p. 355). There are also suggestions of "old-fashioned

bosses" ("pot-bellied and stiff") and "modernistic bosses" ("tanned, thin executives, as 'relaxed' in their conduct as in their manners") (p. 358); there is "the ethical new-wave" which includes executives in the major companies, public or private, and the bosses of large modern, often multinational companies (p. 360), "intellectuals in the old sense" (p. 361), and also "artists" (p. 363). In short, this long chapter is singularly lacking in rigor. The nebulous "dominant class" is never determined or named, and the subcategories constantly change.

Bourdieu goes into details of no interest: was it necessary to point out that: "Private sector executives are definitely more likely (proportionally) to have whisky on their premises while the captains of industry and trade remain most attached to champagne, the traditional drink *par excellence*". This remark is accompanied by a meticulous note on champagne and whisky according to the different categories: private sector executives, engineers, members of the liberal professions, public sector executives, industry owners, commercial leaders, and professors (p. 353), in short, an avalanche of figures for what is well-known — or what is almost nothing at all. Always prolix in justifying the technicality of his language, Bourdieu still uses stereotypes from another time, like "pot-bellied bosses".

This chapter brings little or no new knowledge; the statistics are overwhelming (Bourdieu has a fetish for numbers, and an irrepressible urge for accumulation), the graphs are pretty much unusable, the personal judgments are many, and often very trivial. What is there worth retaining, from this chapter that seems to be made. . . of odds and ends? There doesn't seem to have been much groundwork, but certainly plenty of intensive reading of magazines.

I have placed this criticism in the footnotes because I wanted Bourdieu's comment on the "dominated" to be read well and thus to appear detached. Since Bourdieu reveals and attacks "domination", it is no surprise that he is pitiless in his descriptions of the dominant. But, because he says to want to give the dominated weapons to dominate the domination, we might have expected a sensitive analysis, perhaps sometimes sympathetic, but at least exact and realistic. However, his fantasy view, which he calls objectivation, is unrealistic and without sympathy.

5. "Le sociologue en question", in *Questions de sociologie,* Paris, Editions de Minuit, 1980, p. 41. I borrow this word from Edmond de Goncourt. Returning from a visit to the aging Hugo, he noted that by the pauses in his conversation, his emphases, and his tone, Hugo "made one's attention ache". *Journal,* February 12, 1877.

Chapter IV

Power And Details
In connection with "A Parlor Game", the Appendix to *Distinction* (1979)

Distinction, as we have just shown, is encumbered with minutiae and detailed results the point of which often escapes the reader. Thus, an appendix to *Distinction* leaves me perplexed; I am by no means convinced that the document and its super-interpretation are of any interest. I am talking about the analysis of "a parlor game" (pp. 625-640). In 1975, *Le Point* had commissioned a survey in which a nationally representative sample of respondents was asked to associate various politicians (J. Chirac, V. Giscard d'Estaing, G. Marchais, F. Mitterrand, M. Poniatowski, J.-J. Servan-Schreiber) with just one object from each of several lists: trees, animals, colors, types of hat, flowers, occupations, games, comic strip characters, characters from folk culture, famous detectives, sports champions, famous cars, furniture, women, family members. The researchers told the respondents not to forget that it was a game, which was being played in order to find out more about each of these politicians' images, and that everyone should allow his imagination to run wild.

> The magazine *Sondages* [*Surveys*] (1975, No. 3-4) published the entire set of results, announcing that those who had been polled had expressed "great interest and enjoyment" and that practically nothing had come back "no answer"; the survey respondents had accepted the principle that it was a game and that they should "use [their] imagination". The magazine summed up: "The survey respondents arrived at these associations, most of the time, either by reference to the man's physical aspect, or by reference to his most well-known personality traits or, finally, by reference to his function, his position, and his political career." And it concluded: "We will not comment on these results, leaving it up to reader to allow his own imagination run freely, in turn" (p. 32).

Pierre Bourdieu has always severely criticized polls and pollsters, the biased formulation of their questions and the tendency to subordinate the problem to a particular individual's questions or to political interests, and the significance given to the published results. This survey on politicians was not conducted on the basis of a questionnaire built around the type of problem that might have conformed to Bourdieu's theory. However, he comments on it without hedging, sure that his analysis will be scientific. I should stress that the sample size is not mentioned in the issue of *Sondages* and it does not seem that Bourdieu had any additional information about that — he does not say that he had — nor that he had access to the individual data. He publishes twelve tables aggregating the statistics figures and charts displaying how the six politicians were associated with the objects and the characters, according to the votes (they were to vote for Giscard or Mitterrand), and according to income categories; he also notes that he was able to analyze the distributions by age bracket.

This game is a political game, but Bourdieu underlines, "Make no mistake, [it is political] in a sense that is profound but different from the meaning that the political science institutes and polling institutes give to this word" (p. 627). Then he tells us the meaning of this game: "The politicians, here, are only the pretext for a game of attribution, of *categorization*, and the proposed objects of the attributes, predicates, *categorema* (as Aristotle said, making us forget the original meaning, relevant here, of *accusation*). The question of rules (is that the right word, in this case?), principles or schemas that objectively govern these attributions is objectively posed by the fact that — where one might have expected to note only random associations of the imagination — *statistical regularities* occur that can only be explained if we suppose that. . . in the comparisons that they made, the people questioned were guided by common principles of vision and division" (p. 627). Isn't this an abuse of language? We can observe no "statistical regularities" (since there was only one test) but only associations, of which just a small number are really significant.

Bourdieu authoritatively explains what we must understand for, according to him, the selected significance is "unequivocal" (p. 629). His interpretation, the only one possible, is the product of very dubious assertions. First of all, Bourdieu speaks of statistical regularities where in fact the figures are nearly random. Each time, six names are proposed. If we were following the protocol of random sampling, we know what the margin of error would be. If the probabilities of each box in the table were equal, the average percentage would be 16.6%. The variations would have significance only if they were greater than the margin of error, a margin that depends on the sample size. The authors of the survey suggest that the figures can only be considered noteworthy if they go beyond 30% (thus indicating a rather small sample size). *Sondages*, noting that it would be hard to decipher the many reasons that might lead the respondents to imagine such and such politician as an ant rather than a fox, for example, said that when a politician is associated with one specific object by more than one third of the surveyed, "the explanation is usually immediately clear, and the motivations behind the choices are clear from the various results of the other politicians on the same object" (p. 32).

Pierre Bourdieu, who reminds us that he has never "run away" from the "tasks considered humblest" in the sociologist's job — statistical analysis, for example,[1] takes lightly the constraints of statistics. This attitude is by no means an accidental misstep; Frédéric Bon and Yves Schemeil spoke, almost twenty years ago, of a "curious methodological laxity": "If you pay a little attention when reading Bourdieu's works, you will notice the surprisingly casual way in which he treats the empirical material", and they gave some examples from *A Middle-Brow Art.*[2]

Let's take a close look at the results of the parlor game. For example, Mitterrand and flowers: chrysanthemum, 16%, lily of the valley, 16%, poppy, 21%, narcissus, 17%, lilac, 13%, carnation, 16%. Mitterrand and trees: 16, 16, 17, 21, 15, 17. Or Mitterrand and games: 14, 17, 15, 18, 18, 18.

Poniatowski and games: bridge, 16%, monopoly, 17%, dominos, 21%, poker, 16%, chess, 14%, roulette, 17%. Poniatowski and comic strip characters: 19, 14, 14, 22, 13, 18.

Chirac and famous women: Brigitte Bardot, 21%, Mireille Mathieu, 14%, Jane Birkin, 15%, Michele Morgan, 15%, Jackie Kennedy, 21%, the Queen of England, 15%, etc.. Chirac and animals: 16, 22, 15, 15, 16, 15, etc..

And so on. . . the vast majority of the answers revolves

around the average percentage.

Bourdieu's interpretations seem not to be very sensitive to the value of the statistics. He knows "the meaning" behind a choice. George Marchais was associated by the questionnaire respondents with the color "black" — the other colors suggested being white, blue, yellow, orange, green — and with the crow — the other animals being an ox, ant, cicada, fox, or tortoise. Bourdieu knows what these choices imply: "Black, when one associates it with Marchais, is basically a funeral color, sinister, and probably more specifically, in the dominant representation, a symbol of a pessimistic view of the world (black thoughts from one who sees life blackly); although it is also true that, if you think of the black flag — which could, for some of those surveyed, take the place of the red flag, which was missing from the list — black could take on a positive value, as a symbol of radical subversion. But black is also poverty (black bread, in a French saying), dirtiness (associated with certain trades, like miners — called "black faces"), ignorance (being in the dark), excessive drinking (blacking out), etc." (p. 629). Since Bourdieu strings together ideas that are preconceived, he might have thought, for example, about haute couture, in which he is such a specialist: black also means smart, well-dressed. . .

His interpretation of the color yellow is also contestable: 23% of the surveyed associated it with Jean-Jacques Servan-Schreiber. His diagnosis? The color yellow is "linked to the racist stigmata, the yellow star", and reinforces the choice (by 21%) of the palm tree which is "Israelo-Arabic"; and he talks about a "slight hint of racism" (p. 633). (Another 23% gave Servan-Schreiber orange, but that does not inspire any comment from Bourdieu.)

The oak inspires Bourdieu to exceptionally banal "explanations". The oak is "great and powerful, like a tree in a fable" and Poniatowski "is considered in his corporal *hexis*, powerful and massive". Was it worth the trouble to spell that out, especially given that only 21% of the surveys made this association? Giscard d'Estaing comes out in the lead here, with 31%; in this case, Bourdieu says the oak applies to "social force, power", quite simply to the Head of State.

Bourdieu changes his register when he talks about the fir tree that is associated with George Marchais (by 24% of the survey). The fir is, for me, a tree of beauty and charm, a cheerful tree, associated with Christmas festivals. But, silly me, the fir, here, is not the fir tree, "in its symbolic value or its visible configuration", but the wood. . . Bourdieu points out that fir is a poor quality wood, "used for making coffins" (p. 629). And he explains to us, then, the negative sense of this attribution; the concept noble/ignoble, applied to wood, provides the opposition between the oak ("a noble material used for making beautiful furniture", "a prerogative of [fine] old residences") and the fir tree. I have trouble, once more, following Bourdieu, for 27.1% of the Mitterrand voters link Marchais with the "bad wood" fir tree and 25.9% of those who voted for Giscard do so; why? Since a 1% variation seems to make a difference to Bourdieu, he concludes that George Marchais has a more pejorative "image" among Mitterrand voters than among Giscard voters. Why? Or could it be that the fir does not necessarily have the connotation that he gives it?

Sometimes, Bourdieu distorts the facts. For example, analyzing the images associated with Servan-Schreiber, he concludes that "the idea of ostentation and flashy presentation" is the common denominator of all the choices. He talks about the narcissus, the boater (hat), the cicada (in fact, the tortoise was more often attributed to Servan-Schreiber), the color yellow ("mentioned by the left in particular, no doubt because they are more aware of its . . . connotations; 'yellow' is for those who have betrayed their camp") and the games: heading the list, poker and roulette, which he describes as "games of bluff and the impatience of the *arriviste*" (p. 633). Looking back at the table, one sees: roulette, 26%, and poker, 20%. Offhandedly, between brackets, Bourdieu adds: these games are "attributed" to Chirac as well. We defer to the chart: roulette, 13%, poker,

18%. These statistics amazed me: what Pierre Bourdieu has written is plainly false.[3]

If Bourdieu fudges the figures, he also distorts thoughts. According to him, "those who support the established order" [is this a technical, indispensable paraphrase?], i.e. the Giscard voters, find that Marchais has "pretentious" airs (p. 640). He uses quotation marks here, as if he is making a direct quote; but *none* of the tables of figures reporting the survey results is accompanied by comments. Where does he find that word? Bourdieu the scientist is a wizard who reads minds. . .

One may wonder how he arrives at his comments when he explains the meaning behind the imaginary hat choices. The cap is attributed to Marchais (47%): he states that the cap is "the emblem of the urban hoi polloi" (!) (p. 636); and the beret is associated with Mitterrand (40%): it is "the symbol of the working class moderates, farmers and rural folk". Out of prudence or mistrust, we can double-check the attributions according to the votes (p. 632): among the Giscard voters, 41% associate the beret with Mitterrand, and. . . 41.1% of the Mitterrand voters do so. As for Marchais and his cap: 53.3% of Mitterrand voters surveyed ascribe it to him, while 46% of the Giscard voters do so. Maybe the Mitterrand voters think of him more in terms of the "urban hoi polloi"?! and are more scornful of the cap than are "the supporters of the established order"?!

Bourdieu calls our attention to two attributes of "statutory competence": education level and gender. He makes some remarks on the choices according to the gender of the surveyees. Women are less politicized, so they allow themselves to be led by analogies with nonpolitical traits of the personality, for example, the corporal *hexis*, which is presently "complimentarily" by the women's magazines, "e.g. as for Poniatowski, the prince will overtake the Interior Minister" (p. 631). Unfortunately, Bourdieu, who is never miserly in his comments, does not provide any statistics breaking down the choices according to sex; I look at the attributions, and the social portrait of Poniatowski leaves me in a daze. We find: ox, helmet, armoire, father, Peugeot 504, the Queen of England, and the other statistics are not decisive. . . Does the prince really come out ahead of the Interior Minister?

Bourdieu is does not hold back, either, as you might suspect, on his considerations on the men's political competence. Thus, people more frequently thought of the ant in conjunction with Giscard, because they know that he was a Finance Minister; in fact, Bourdieu teaches us this with great care. "The idea of hoarding and saving, which the ant evokes — through the contrast to the grasshopper, and La Fontaine's fable — is only associated with Giscard (just like the link with the movie *The Miser*, which varies according to same logic) if one knows that he worked in the Finance Ministry" (!). And if the men give "lawyer" as a trade for Mitterrand, it is "undoubtedly" because they know his profession better; and if they think of chess when it comes to Marchais, it is "by the mediation" of the high esteem that the USSR accorded chess players, whereas the women undoubtedly "see" it as an intellectual game and thus associate it more strongly with Giscard...

These details surely annoy you, and me, but it takes patience to see what Bourdieu is playing at, to show his taste for rambling on about minor or obvious facts. When he criticizes those who criticize him, he attacks those who reproach him for stating the obvious and for falsehoods: he calls this evidence of "formidable resistance" to sociological analysis, on the part of erroneous readers, and he talks about the pot calling the kettle black, and Freud[4]... I maintain that he makes *false statements* (see above, and how he says that Chirac is associated with games of bluff) *and* of sententious *banalities*; for example, his comments on the oak are as dull as can be, and his remarks on men's politicization are of no interest.

Bourdieu assures us that each of the figures comes out with "a sociologically coherent social portrait". This is certainly true for Giscard d'Estaing: oak, bridge (the game), top hat, Rolls-Royce, and Louis XVI armchair are attributions one would make to a president of the French Republic. But Jacques Chirac? None of the associations barely reached 30%, so the portrait is fuzzy. And the same holds true for François Mitterrand, except for the beret, R5, and the occupation of lawyer. . . As for Marchais, he is well drawn: black, poppy, crow, cap, the 2CV (an extremely modest car), a farm-kitchen table, Mireille Mathieu, concierge, Popeye, and cousin.[5] Bourdieu sees this as a pejorative portrait. Admittedly, the crow[6] is not a flattering attribute, but many of these features are simply popular and are not pejorative; and besides, isn't George Marchais a son of the people, and proud of it? Now, you do see that the question of the rules, the principles and the concepts that govern these attributions is "objectively" posed, don't you? Is all that convincing?

Of course, and how! For Bourdieu makes a point of giving us the meaning of this survey, a meaning that, perhaps, you have not yet discerned. "Imbued with the hierarchies that they impose, because these hierarchies are imposed on them, the authors of the questionnaire have produced, in the guise of a game (which eliminates any censure), a set of 'data' which can be taken *just as it is, in all objectivity*, to produce a political effect" (p. 627).

What political effect does he see, here? In this game

without censure, one sees Mireille Mathieu associated with George Marchais (36%), and very seldom the Queen of England or Jackie Kennedy (8% in both cases), and as a hat, the cap (as was already mentioned) (47%), and not the top hat (4%) (p. 626). Bourdieu says: that's the trick! "A 'majority' associates the most pejorative attributes with the representatives of the Left, and especially Marchais," (p. 627). And when the respondents attribute dominated professions to dominant people (Mitterrand voters, who see Poniatowski as a concierge — 31.2%, and Chirac as a hairdresser — 21.5%), aren't they "dreaming of *lowering* the dominant ones by imposing this on them with the intent of taking symbolic revenge?" (p. 640 7.) Bourdieu comments that the symmetry between the intention of making Poniatowski and Chirac into concierges and hairdressers, and this "kind of role reversal proposed by the partisans of the established order, by assigning Mitterrand or Marchais — and especially the latter . . . — to places that seem to suit them by nature" (p. 640) is only an apparent symmetry.

Thus, Bourdieu comments on everything that goes his way (and in that case, he remarks upon the slightest detail, or he "bends" the statistics in his favor, to make them support his theoretical diagram, to show that "When it comes to classifying objects that are *socially classified and classifying*, i.e. unequally *distributed* between the social classes and, consequently, unequally *associated* with the social classes in implicit and explicit comparisons, we observe the same accord on the significance associated to the same discord on the value of the things classified" (p. 635).

The comments on the statistics are tiresome to read, and you may wonder whether they were truly necessary. It may be that our boredom has to do with the fact that only a vision as powerful as that of this savant can synthesize so much detail. . . But Bourdieu is certain that this labor is of interest and does not neglect to remind us of that in his sidebars: "One might say that the attributions people make are guided by a social sense that is a quasi-sociology, a practical and quite well-founded intuition, of the correspondence between social positions and tastes."[8]

It is worth discussing Bourdieu's comments on this parlor game, for in just a few pages he pulls together all the usual characteristics of his sociology: methodological laxity, the purportedly scientific use of a survey that made no claim to be scientific, a curious way of reading the statistics, dogmatic and groundless comments, and comments that are no less dogmatic and no less like weed-like, spilling over into topics of no interest — in short, political discourse camouflaged as science. It also shows his imperialist view of science, a view that postulates that everything is an object of scientific sociology. And every opinion that he emits, for example his remarks on the meaning of the colors "black" and "yellow", are scientific statements.

The subject that he deals with here bears only the faintest relation with the purported subject. Was this analysis of the "animal, vegetable or mineral" game of portraiture really necessary in order to arrive at a reformulation of all the traditional questions on the beautiful, on art, taste, and culture? — That is the subject of his book, don't forget.

This work displays all the least acceptable aspects of Pierre Bourdieu's sociology: the imposition of opinions as though they were "indisputable" results — any criticism is really a matter of "resistance" — and especially the way he reduces the world to social classes and classifications, to the classifications of objects that are socially classified and which classify those associated with them, etc. — in short, Bourdieu's bitter fantasy world.

Footnotes

1. *Méditations pascaliennes,* Paris, le Seuil, 1997, p. 13.
2. Frédéric Bon, Yves Schemeil, "La rationalisation de l'inconduite. Comprendre le statut du politique chez Pierre Bourdieu", *Revue française de science politique,* XXX, No 6, December 1980, p. 1205.
   In connection with *Un art moyen,* Frédéric Bon and Yves Schemeil wrote in a note: "There is no end to the hasty quotes and stretched interpretations which one would like to believe are the result of a desire to do well. Here is one such naive formula, among others: 'Young people (say) they are interested in opinion polls" more often than older ones (26% of the under-49 versus 23% of the 50-64 age group and 19% of the 65-and-up), p. 1206.
3. Not wanting to transgress "the principle of charity", often recalled by the charitable Bourdieu, I then looked at the table of "games" choices according to the vote: the Mitterrand voters associate with Chirac: poker, 24.3% and roulette, 17.8%. Even while offering him this escape route, I see that Bourdieu reads hastily, and does a lot of interpreting.
4. "Une science qui dérange", *Questions de sociologie,* Paris, Editions de Minuit, 1980, p. 56 (republication of an interview published in *Recherche,* under the title: "Is sociology a science?").
5. One question required respondents to classify each politician as: a son, father-in-law, brother, son-in-law, father, or cousin; this, says Bourdieu, is "a way of expressing social or political proximity and distance" (p. 635). [Did he really have to tell us that, wouldn't we have understood?] Marchais was classified as cousin or rather "shunted off", said Bourdieu, with the sons-in-law, cousins or fathers-in-law, i.e. relatives "whom one prefers to keep at a distance". Some Mitterrand voters also made Marchais a cousin, but they especially did not make him a son or a son-in-law.
6. The crow is "a bird of ill omen", says Bourdieu. The Mitterrand voters associated Chirac with the crow (28%; for the whole of the population, it is 16%).
7. Bourdieu wrote: ". . . making a chauffer or a concierge out of

Poniatowski, Chirac, or, not without hesitations, Giscard. . ." (p. 640). The Mitterrand voters see Giscard as a chauffeur (20.6%), much less as a hairdresser (13.1%) and even less concierge (9.3%): Bourdieu says that this figure indicates an attribution "not without hesitations" (!): here again, we see that Bourdieu forgets the average percentage. . .

8. "The paradox of the sociologist", Conference given in Arras (Noroit), in October 1977, in *Questions de sociologie, op. cit.,* p. 91. The text on "the Chinese game" published in the appendix to *Distinction* had been published before in *Actes de la recherche en sciences sociales,* August 1976, 2nd year, No. 4, pp. 91-101.

Chapter V
Does Bourdieu Understand Bourdieu?
On his works on School and on *Homo Academicus* (1984)

In *An Invitation to Reflexive Sociology* (1992), Pierre Bourdieu speaks on several occasions about *Homo Academicus.* This is, he said, "the culmination, at least in the biographical sense, of a kind of 'epistemological experimentation' which I began, quite consciously, in the early 1960's, when I applied to a familiar universe the methods of investigation which I had used earlier to uncover the logic of the relations of kinship in a foreign universe. . . ". And, further: ". . . I have never left off seeing myself as an object of study, not in a narcissistic sense, but as a representative of a category. I never irritate other people so much as when I analyze myself — *Homo Academicus* contains pages and pages about myself, in that I analyze categories to which I belong; in which, in speaking about myself, I tell the truth about the others by proxy. . . "[2] Dwelling on this "personal" book, Bourdieu was supported by Loïc J. D. Wacquant who vouchsafed that, of all his books, this was the one that cost Bourdieu "the most effort" and also the greatest "concern".[3]

These assertions intrigued me, probably because I had not noticed any evidence of such effort, especially since the book had hardly left any traces in my memory. The way the author celebrates this book has led me to read again his works on School, which always elicited many criticisms from every political corner. To these critics who wanted to open a discussion, Bourdieu always retorted contemptuously that he did not want to waste his time, for he could not hope "to reduce, by logical refutation, remarks whose lack of logic is evidence enough that they can only be entertained and accepted because they are based on sociological reasons that are more powerful than any logical reason". However, he admitted that his first works had been produced under certain historical conditions that might "sometimes have inclined [him] to 'twist the stick in the other direction' to fight the ideology of 'school as an emancipator'. . .".[4]

Were the historical conditions the only factor that might explain his pessimistic research, undertaken as a battle, or had he not rather ignored certain essential characteristics of school? Here, he acknowledges the ideological character of his work. He wanted to debunk what appeared to him to be a myth; he was not looking to analyze the contradictions of School, the in fact inextricable tangle of the progressivists and the conservatives. He was looking to produce a proof that would support his own conviction.

> Being interested in the ideological nature of the entire work, I was enlightened by re-reading his texts on Algeria for the ideology there is only slightly masked: this is probably explained by the youth of the author, the historical circumstances of the time, and his political choices, the brevity of his visit and a new-found knowledge. Since he had gone with the idea of denouncing the colonists and the "Europeans", Bourdieu took up the defense of all the human relations, the customs, the morals, the sense of honor, etc. (and why not polygamy. . .) of the Arabic-speaking people, the Kabyles, the M'zabites. . . Indeed, it is not the few pages on colonial society that require an attentive reading, but as a particularly conclusive example, his description and his rehabilitation of the *khammessat* —whereby the *khammès* receives *a fifth of the harvest.* In a tone that pretends to be "factual" and objective, these remarks take on the appearance of research. When General Governor Jacques Soustelle looked into the institution of the *khammessat,* he saw serfdom, the imposition of intolerable economic conditions; and he set out to bring it to an end. When Bourdieu arrived in Algeria, the *khammessat* was already banned, and the *khammès* had become for the most part sharecroppers or farm workers. From where did he get his views on it? He describes the *khammessat* as being a consummate model of man's relations with man.

"The *khammès* contributes his material services, the master contributes his spiritual services." "The pact is an arrangement between man and man, and there is no other guarantee than the 'fidelity' required by honor. The unilateral character of the relationship is moderated by the pressure of prompt public opinion that rejects any abuse by the master. There is no abstract discipline or specific sanction. The pact is maintained and supported by pride and the fear of reprobation. Because he would be in default if he failed to do his part, the tenant remains faithful to the master. For the same reason, if he feels he has been oppressed or exploited, he can denounce him and the pressure of public opinion will require the great ones to show that they are worthy of their rank. . . magnanimity and generosity constitute not only attributes of grandeur but virtues that naturally redound to him. . . The worker participates intimately in the family group and he shares its concerns, sorrows and sometimes misery, their interests are his interests, he sees himself as being 'associated' with them. . . This contract seems to be built on the model of a deeper relation, that which links father and son, [and] the master engages in fact to ensure the subsistence of the *khammès* and to relieve him of all worries about the future. Doesn't the *khammèsat* provide the best protection and the best insurance? Protected from poverty, the *khammès* is also protected against isolation. . . ." Bourdieu then reveals the advantages to the master. "Wealth is prized not so much in its own right or for the material satisfactions that it ensures as for the enrichment in prestige and influence that comes with having a 'clientele', a human entourage which is like the projection of a protective force. The owner finds it to his advantage, although it appears he is losing out if we only look at the question of economic profitability, because the pact is above all an exchange of honor and prestige. . . ." Bourdieu admits, however, that there may be a secret temptation to "exploitation and parasitism".[5] The

> *khammessat*, the way he imagines it, is as beautiful as that affectionate, protective slavery, woven of fidelity and generosity, depicted in *Gone with the Wind.*
>
> Bourdieu knew what he wanted to show when he began his research. When you know where you want to end up, it is easy to choose the parts of reality that lead in the desired direction, or in this specific case, to make an interpretation that is indifferent to reality. It is astonishing that Bourdieu, who considers himself the author of works devoted to tracking, revealing, and explaining all the forms of symbolic violence that help to found, reproduce and transform the structures of domination, sees the *khammessat* — an overt form of domination — as a consummate model of relations between men.

Reproduction (1970) is a good example of the militant aspect of Bourdieu's sociology; he always knows, from the outset, where he wants to end up. Probably because of his own background, so often cited, he felt a certain uneasiness with regard to school; it did not seem to him to match up to the ideal of school as a liberating institution.

One work led him to say that school contributed to reproducing the structure of the distribution of cultural capital between the classes and thereby to reproducing the established relations between the classes. A sociological approach should have seen, and said, that school partly contributes to this reproduction, but that it also fulfills many other roles. The abrupt title of the book, *Reproduction*, the writing that outraged thoughtful minds, did everything possible to give the impression that this aspect represented the entire effect of the education system. Since then, Bourdieu has never stopped claiming that he is being misread. However, his own stubbornness or blindness lies at the heart of this reception, because he took one part for the whole picture, one shortcoming for the whole story, and that shortcoming for the truth. School, in the history of the people, of the classes, is not only that which he claims to reveal and to denounce.[6]

And his indictment of school does not stop there. School does more than reproduce privileges, it destroys the values of the dominated social sectors — farm-country values, for example. This ideology is openly displayed in "Prohibited Reproduction" (1989), an article in which he takes up the problem of the rural bachelor.

> His dialogue with Loïc J. D. Wacquant was the thing that most induced me to read this article. He said: "The case of bachelorhood is interesting, because it has to do with an extremely important economic phenomenon: France liquidated a very large proportion of its peasants in thirty years without the least police violence (except for putting down demonstrations), whereas the Soviet Union employed the most violent means to liquidate its farming community." He added that he had said that in his article, "in a much more respectable way".[7] Without wishing to take too much time, I'd like to make a point of underlining all that is fallacious in this comparison, and how much its militant tone exposes his "scientific ap-

> proach". It is strange that, while he asserts the need for "technical" terms and periphrases, he resorts to the expression: "France liquidated"; and "France" is an odd concept, anyway.

The article talks about the role of education in the loss of values, the crisis of rural values society, and the celibacy of the rural populace. True, he says: "The correlation between the level of schooling and the declining marriage rate among farmers. . . should not be read as a causal relationship", the two trends being "products of the same principle".[8] On several occasions he returns to the role of the prolongation of compulsory schooling, of the lengthening of studies: this experience "tends to make the values transmitted by the family less real", in particular for girls. "Deculturation takes place especially easily among girls, whose aspirations always tend to be organized around marriage and who are, therefore, more sensitive to urban fashions and manners and to the ensemble of social markers that define the value of potential partners on the market of symbolic goods" (p. 32). Deculturation is, among other things, the rift that studying causes, in lifestyle, in the temporal rhythms of country life, and "the progressively declining acceptability of the vernacular language" (p. 30). Education leads girls to be "impressed, and docile with regard to urban injunctions or seductions". "Less attached than the men (and the young men) to country life and less engaged in the work and in the responsibilities of power, therefore less caught up in concerns over the patrimony to be "maintained", more disposed toward education and the promises of mobility that it offers, they import into the heart of the rural world the city viewpoint that devalues and discredits 'rural qualities'" (p. 24). Thus women, who are looking more and more toward the city, "feel reluctant to marry a peasant who promises them exactly that which they are trying to flee. . . Finally, and especially, they are more likely to find a mate outside the rural world. . ." (p. 27).

This shows how conservative Bourdieu's view can be, calling to mind the preachers of a back-to-the-land movement, Joseph de Pesquidoux or Gustave Thibon, for example. The education system destroys the culture and produces "aspirations" toward town life, which is an "abandonment" of country "values" (the interests of "the house", and its assets. . .), and through this dispossession, it imposes the legitimacy of domination. "School fulfills its function as an instrument of symbolic domination, contributing to the conquest of a new market for the symbolic products of the city; and while it does not manage to provide the means of adopting the dominant culture, it can at least inculcate a recognition of the legitimacy of this culture and of those who have the means of adopting it" (p. 31).

So, in his works on education, Bourdieu mentions school only in connection with the reproduction of privileges for one side, and in connection with a rupture, loss, pain, and disorientation for the others. Read the last lines of *Reproduction*: "Thus, in a society where obtaining social privileges depends more and more closely on having academic degrees, school only serves the function of ensuring the discreet succession rights of the bourgeoisie, which can no longer be transmitted directly and overtly. Schooling is a favorite instrument of bourgeois social dictatorship that confers on the privileged the supreme privilege of not appearing to be privileged, and it is easy to convince the poor that they owe their scholastic and social destiny to their lack of talents or merits, since when it comes to culture, absolute dispossession precludes one's awareness of the dispossession.[9]

At the beginning of *Homo Academicus*, Bourdieu announces that it will be a treatise on academic passions (p. 16); in fact, the passions are related to very few things, primarily to the search for forms of power, forms of profit. In his respectful commentary on *An Invitation to Reflexive Sociology*, George Balandier did express one regret. "We must also measure the price that is paid for reaching the state of scientific sociology promoted by Bourdieu. The place conceded to desire, to the past, to appearances, to the shortcomings of rationality can only be scantly measured."[10] It should be clearly stated that if Bourdieu believes he is promoting a scientific sociology, it is at the price of a drastic reduction of the world: the world that he analyzes is boiled down to just a few dimensions, always the same ones, and certainly not the passions.[11]

University professors, the supreme academics, place their capital in the university arena and play delicately (silently, before 1968), to obtain, increase or maintain: power, prestige, domination, social success, etc.. In Bourdieu's view, the university field is not a select club, even though he talks about a "diffuse and imperceptible complicity", p. 197, but a corporative trade union (even before the Autonomous Union was created in 1968). The sociologist only looks at recruitment, career standards and profiles, promotion criteria, and the increased or decreased value attributed to advanced degrees. There is nothing wrong with all that, although it is often of scant interest; if that is all that interests the sociologist, he should say so instead of claiming to reveal and explain the university world. The first chapter is boldly called "A 'Book to Burn'?" (a book that hoped to be burned?). Who would have had such an impulse? All you have to do with this book is put it down. The only thing about it that might be aggravating is not its audacity, but its unpleasant quirks and its methodological laxity.

This book contains, as usual, considerations on the courage of the true sociologist: "The sorcerer's apprentice who takes the risk of showing an interest in indigenous sorcery and its fetishes, instead of going off to seek the reassuring charms of an exotic magic under distant tropical skies, must expect to see the violence that he unleashes being turned on him" (p. 15). The author takes the time to tell us of the difficulties that he encountered and overcame in attaining scientific knowledge, the problems of communicating such knowledge (the problems of writing[12]), the "resistance" put up by readers who are related to the institution of the university: "To understand, in this case, is difficult only because one understands only too well, in a certain manner, and one *wants* neither to see nor to know that which one understands" (p. 52). Bourdieu challenges flawed readings, misreadings, and wrong analyses, real or potential, in advance. He speaks for the thousandth time about the work the researcher must do on himself in order to try to objectify everything that links him to the object of study, an effort that the reader must "replicate on his own account in order to master the social principles of interest that might get in his way while he is reading" (p. 48).

> We must not overlook, here, that which he has so often and so lengthily pointed out, on the job that the observer under observation must perform if he is to be likely to

> succeed. "The most critical sociology is that which supposes and implies the most radical self-criticism, and the objectification of the one who is objectifying is both a condition and a product of complete objectification: the sociologist has a chance of being successful in his task of objectification only if, as an observer being observed, he subjects to objectification not only all that he is — his own social conditions of production and thereby 'the boundaries of his brain', but also his own effort of objectification, the hidden interests that are invested there, and the profits that they promise."[13] [(!) Careful, you may need to re-read this portion. . .]

One could tolerate such manias if they were founded on solid empirical material. In connection with the "parlor game", I referred to material that was not very interesting and that was, moreover, mishandled. In *Homo Academicus*, the material itself has been collected in a heterogeneous, often arbitrary way; many of the indicators are debatable, for example, the *Palmes Académiques* [an award for services to education, the arts or sciences], as one of "the indicators of the capital of power in the university world", television broadcasts as indicators of "the capital of intellectual recognition", etc..

Far worse, religion is listed among the demographic indicators and indicators of inherited or acquired capital, with four categories: Jews, Protestants, "known Catholics", and others. How do you define a "known" Catholic? In presenting the collected data, Bourdieu wrote that "to avoid" any "distortions, dissimulations and deformations" and to avoid "being suspected or accused of religious cataloguing or of conducting a police investigation", he had taken the position "of working exclusively from information that was *public or intended for publication*" (the words are in italics, p. 60). I was surprised to find the designation *known Catholics*, and even more, to find the label "*Jew*". In presenting the indicators, Bourdieu makes references to "the family's original religion"; is he talking about families that are "known" to be Jewish? practicing Jews? or of Jewish identity, a term that he sometimes uses? Whom has he lumped together under this label and on what basis? He talks about *public* information. Then, in which public information did he find the percentage of Jewish professors in the sciences, in literature, law, medicine? (p. 66.) This problem is very complex and delicate; yet Bourdieu hardly pays any attention to that, because his view of the world is already fully formed. For example, he affirms that Jews and known Catholics occupy the two opposite ends of the spectrum in the space organized under the twin relations of economic capital and intellectual capital and the correlative relations to these two types of capital. "An affinity between the heretical or critical dispositions of those who occupy socially dominated and intellectually dominant positions, and the critical ruptures associated with the scientific practice, especially in the social sciences; the affinity between the disposition of the man of order (did you think it is by chance that these positions of order are so often filled by officers' sons?), of orthodoxy, right-leaning or on the right, in a social world that so obviously conforms to the expectations that appear self-evident, and the inseparably middle-class and Catholic denial of science, with all the troublesome critical, heretical questions and conundrums that it raises, which so often directs the natural-born scientists "in particular those from the Polytechnic School" toward the areas of thought where physics and metaphysics, biology and spiritism, archaeology and theosophy meet" (p. 75).

It is clear why Bourdieu mixes together his empirical material without too much concern, for his conclusions (that is, his opinions) do not need to decode any empirical material. The "bourgeois denial of science" would be hard to prove, in our day and age. . .

It is not to save paper that he omits any analyses and probative examples. As for his opinion on those natural-born scientists who head into *those areas of thought such as physics and metaphysics, etc.* — where would one look to find any evidence or indications that might justify his ratiocinations? We might also ask him to define what he calls a "man of order". In short, he delivers his personal impressions as if they were scientific reports.

What is there worth remembering, in this book? What are its "assets"? Certainly not the explanation of the crisis of May 1968, since it describes the crisis as though it had unfolded entirely within a closed field, outside of the real world immersed in history. After going on about the coed population, the increasing levels of schooling and the increase in student enrollments, the increase in jobs, career acceleration and its effects, he comes to the "critical moment": the new disciplines and the challenges of getting a start in them (and also a new student profile, in sociology for example), the subordinate levels looking ahead to a stagnant future, the gap between the statutory aspirations and the guaranteed opportunities . . .

Having taken a close look at the guaranteed futures and the arrested futures, he stresses that after a certain time, the fault line was drawn between the professors and the teaching assistants and assistant professors who, objectively speaking, are for the most part closer to the students than to the full professors. Then he delivers his analysis, not only of the crisis of May 1968, but of the model of revolutionary processes. "This disruption of the *chain of anticipated identifications*, founded in the order of the successions which they tend to reproduce, naturally encourages a kind of secession of the agents who, excluded from the race for the future that had been, until then, pre-ordained for them due to their positions, are driven to question the race itself. And in this we can no doubt recognize one particular manifestation of a general model of the revolutionary processes: the objective rupture of the circle of hopes and opportunities leads a large fraction of the least dominated among the dominated (here, the intermediate categories of the teaching staff; elsewhere, the petty bourgeoisie) to opt out of the race, that is, the competition, where participation implies acknowledging the game and the stakes posed by the dominant, and to join in a fight that can be called revolutionary insofar as it aims to institute other goals and thus to more or less completely redefine the game and the attributes that would enable one to triumph there" (pp. 225-226).

Pierre Bourdieu describes a poor mechanical model: iron men, without souls, without flesh, programmed, caught up in dual confrontations. If *Homo Academicus*, published in 1984, faded from my memory, it is not because I rejected the shocking discoveries unveiled therein, but because those discoveries appeared to me to be very small in scope compared to the promised scope of the project. If I have spoken brutally about this book that the author esteems so highly, it is because, fundamentally, the gist of the book is that *Homo academicus* = *academica mediocritas*, which is nothing more than a pundit's pronouncement. What he calls objectification is, in fact, more like the results of a viewpoint like that of *Le Canard enchâiné* or the *Guignols de l'information* produces.

> It is interesting to note that *Libération* published a laudatory article, "*Le Canard enchâiné*, From Political Satire to Defending Public Morality", which exposes how Bourdieu and company confound sociology and "morality", which leads him to approve of practices that are more a matter of denunciation than of observation and analysis.
>
> The journalists of *Le Canard enchâiné*, wrote Patrick Champagne, practice a very serious form of investigative journalism; their sources are highly authoritative: high-ranking civil servants, politicians, and journalists who could not write these things in their own newspapers. . . who wish to see "an injustice denounced, to point a finger at certain absurdities or to reveal a scandal". (So, high-ranking civil servants who, for example, "tattle on" other people and who do not follow the deontologic rules of their profession and of their status, have their good reasons.) "By shifting the boundary between the politics on display and that which is going on behind closed doors, the locus of personal and often inadmissible competition, and in seeking to denounce 'scandals', i.e. those actions in which a position of power, which is supposed to be occupied in order to serve in a disinterested way, is diverted to private ends, to serve someone's private interests, this weekly contributes, in its own way, to promoting what one might call 'public morality'."[14]

Bourdieu, who proclaims that his work is both useful and effective, sees himself as a righter of wrongs. Is he looking to promote public morality? That's a curious job for an intellectual. At the time, I had thought that his supporting Coluche in the 1981 presidential elections was a mistake[15]; in fact, this action falls well within his worldview and the idea of power that he wants to have. Now I understand better his repetitive pages, describing his efforts, his courage, the risks he has taken, the "challenges" he has raised, "the fight — perhaps lost before it began" against disproportionate social forces, and the sadness that runs through the *Pascalian Meditations*. . . He was in the wrong century, and in the wrong role. The intellectual's job is more modest, and more discreet than that.

Footnotes

1. Pierre Bourdieu, with Loïc J. D. Wacquant, *Réponses. Pour une anthropologie réflexive,* Paris, le Seuil, 1992, p. 47. Bourdieu is referring to his work on celibacy and the rural condition in Béarn, succeeding his work on marriage in Kabylia.
2. *Ibid,* p. 175.
3. *Ibid,* p. 45.
4. "Classement, déclassement, reclassement", *Actes de la recherche en sciences sociales*, No. 24, November 1978, p. 22. "Bourdieu is very considtent in his ideas *on the reception of one's œuvre, for example:* It is understood that writers' efforts to control the reception of their own work are always partially doomed to failure; even if only because the effect of their *œuvre* itself can transform how it is received and they would not have had to write a number of things that they wrote and would not have had to write them the way they wrote them, for example, resorting to rhetorical strategies aiming 'to twist the stick in the other direction' — if they had been granted from the start what one grants them retrospectively." [Which writers is Bourdieu talking about? A poet who twists the stick in the other direction? or a sociologist?] "Le champ littéraire," *Actes de la recherche en sciences sociales*, No. 89, September 1991, p. 20.
5. *Sociologie de l'Algérie,* Paris, PUF, "Que sais-je?", 1961, pp. 68-70.
6. In 1993, in "*La Misère du monde,*" Bourdieu finally moderated his views on School: for young immigrants, the school verdict confirms their exclusion, but School is also the opportunity to discover and to enjoy their full membership in French society (and also more or less explicitly to imbue the democratic culture that generates universalist aspirations, such as the rejection of racism." Paris, Editions de Minuit, p. 225.
7. Pierre Bourdieu, with Loïc J.D. Wacquant, "*Réponses. Pour une anthropologie réflexive,*" *op. cit*, p. 141.
8. Pierre Bourdieu, "Reproduction interdite. La dimension symbolique de la domination économique", *Études rurales*, Nos 113-114, January-June 1989, p. 31.
9. *Réproduction, Eléments pour une théorie du système d'ensei-*

gnement, in collaboration with Jean-Claude Passeron, Paris, Editions de Minuit, 1970, p. 253.

10. George Balandier, "Le pari de Bourdieu", *Le Monde*, January 24, 1992.
11. It all seems the same. Does the model of *Distinction* apply to the GDR? Bourdieu answers in *15 jours avant la chute du Mur de Berlin.* We need to examine, he says, the principles of differentiation characteristic of this society. In France, it is economic capital and cultural capital that have significant influence on the structure of social space. In the GDR there is another species of capital, political capital, which is the collective resources made into the public heritage. Bourdieu explains contemporary conflicts in the GDR with great tact: he sees them as originating in the impatience of those who hold educational capital vis-à-vis those who have political capital. He wondered whether the intellectuals, those who dream of a "true socialism", would be able "to establish a real, and especially long lasting, alliance with the dominated", i.e. manual workers or even "the lower-rung employees of State bureaucracies". He saw very clearly "the immediately satisfactions" that ordinary capitalism offered and he announced that they were "laden with obvious risks".

    "The 'Soviet' Alternative and Political Capital", a conference given in East Berlin on October 25, 1989, *Raisons pratiques*, Paris, le Seuil, 1994, pp. 31-35.

    Every society is reduced to the same dimensions; Bourdieusian sociology makes one think of Bainvillian history which was fixed in observing the immutable repetitions of History. The sociology of Pierre Bourdieu, despite all his denials, is deterministic (and pessimist).
12. "Scientific discourse differs from the discourse of fiction — the novel, for example, which is given more or less openly as a pretend, fictitious discourse, in that (as John Searle notes) it *means to say* what it says, it takes what it says seriously and will answer for it, i.e., if necessary, to be convinced of any error", p. 43. Here, finally, is a reasonable proposition.
13. "Sur l'objectivation participante. Réponse à quelques objections", *Actes de la recherche en sciences sociales*, No 23, September 1978, p. 68.
14. Patrick Champagne, *Le Canard enchâiné*, de la satire politique à la défense de la morale publique", *Actes de la re-*

cherche en sciences sociales, No. 89, September 1991, *Liber, p. 8.*

Publishing an investigation into the Bourdieusian networks, *Libération* (April 16, 1998) gives us this researcher's state of mind: Look at the current success of *Charlie Hebdo. . .* We are of the same mind: we want to be there, to say what we think, to refuse consensus, to play at being bloody nuisances." Which does not prevent him from foolishly affirming: *And we stick to the most scientific approach possible.*

15. The appeal wrote, among other things: "Popularity, humor and virulence against those [Coluche] who denounce the degradation of the state of freedom and of conditions in France can attract million of abstentions on principle and also voters who can no longer recognize themselves in the traditional parties, at least in their leaders", *Le Monde*, November 20, 1980). Bourdieu, who is constantly saying that he takes so much trouble to write the way one must write, scientifically, technically, rigorously, was content in 1980 to talk about "the degradation of the state of freedom". *Is that really a rigorous thought?*

Chapter VI

War Without Peace

On *The Rules of Art* (1992)

The illusion of knowledge without limits is never belied so clearly as in X's analysis of Flaubert's writings, in which he reveals the limits to how well one can comprehend another intellectual, i.e., oneself as an intellectual (p. 293).

In 1994, introducing a collection of speeches that he had presented to audiences abroad to prove the universal validity of the models that he had constructed using the case of France as a basis, Pierre Bourdieu explained that this was the essence of his work, "its most elementary and fundamental level", and that this "essence often escaped readers and commentators"; "it's probably my fault", he added.

In fact, he did not say where he was "at fault" or how he shared in the blame for "reductive" readings, but he took the trouble to denounce "the misplaced point of (spiritual) honor" on the part of readers who resisted sociological analysis and he summarized "the essence" of his work: a philosophy of *relational* science, "in that it gives primacy to relations", "objective relations" that one can neither prove nor put a finger on, and that it is neces-

> sary to apprehend, construct and validate through scientific work"; and a philosophy of *dispositional* action which notes the potentialities registered in the corps of the agents and the structure of the situations in which they act or, more precisely, in their relations", a philosophy condensed into a small number of fundamental concepts, the *habitus*, the field, and capital".[1]

The structure of his huge book, *The Rules of Art*, has eluded many readers, and that is certainly *his fault*. The book pulls together a great many articles, and claims to be intended to found a science of cultural productions.[2] Of all of Bourdieu's books, this one is surely the most difficult to follow. He constantly changes register, in his writing, between "technical language" and "ordinary language"; he repeats himself all the time (reprising his earlier texts as well as earlier parts of the book); and he openly contradicts the conclusions of his earlier works on culture.[3] He makes dubious assimilations to science and uses them in place of proofs. He presents a heterogeneity of information covering the 19th century, crisscrossing all sorts of terrain without explaining how it all fits together.[4] He cites arbitrarily selected comparisons,[5] offers a proliferation of personal judgments that he affirms as being scientific, grants "On the Question of Method" a prominent position in the middle of the book (pp. 249-296), and introduces his "Parerga and paralipomena" — the "neglected context of the text". What is the result? Hardly anything, except for unproven assertions, and suggestions of trails that should be followed, research projects that should be undertaken.

Bourdieu says he feels a certain annoyance when he reads works that venture off into the territory of "grand theories" (p. 249). I hereby acknowledge that I feel very annoyed indeed when I read this book, full as it is of theoretical remarks and practically devoid of empirical research, with avalanches of comments, questions of method, and innumerable recommendations: *what should be done* — "an analysis should be made. . .", "this should be demonstrated. . ." , "only a well-constructed chronicle could show. . .", etc.. And more irritating yet is the "dissymmetrical relation" which he feels authorized to establish (with philosophers as well as with writers and sociologists, past and present) and the notion that he intends "to think better than they have thought, by making the experience of the intellectual and his social status into the special target of an analysis which [he] believes to be perfectly lucid".[6] Since he concentrates in one being a whole battery of abilities that are not generally found in one individual, he expresses open contempt for literature professors: "*A Sentimental Education*, that work that has been critiqued a thousand times, and probably never really read", which, however, "provides all the instruments necessary to its own sociological analysis: the structure of the work, which a strictly *internal reading* brings to light, i.e. the structure of the social space in which Frederic's adventures unfold, is also the structure of the social space in which the author himself is located". This structure "seems obvious, once it has barely been stated, and it has escaped the most attentive interpreters" (p. 19).

Before him, nobody knew how to read, and so nobody had understood. His book is full of advice and acerbic criticism, and makes a point of setting itself apart, of *distinguishing itself*.[7]

"The partial objectifications of the polemic or the satire are just as formidable an obstacle as the narcissistic complacency of projective criticism", he writes. "Those who produce these instruments of combat camouflaged as instruments of analysis forget that they should apply them first to that part of themselves that belongs to the objectified category" (p. 271). If Bourdieu would apply his pages of combat to himself, or quite simply keep them to himself, perhaps that would help us to read his writings; it is the overwhelming proportion of his writing that is dedicated to put-downs that governs how his writings are received.

Before we turn to the heart of his book, we should repeat that he gives the reader many reasons to smile to himself. "The illusion of the absolute power of a thought that can be, in itself, its only basis, must be part of the same disposition as the ambition to dominate, without sharing, the intellectual field" (p. 267). Is this, for once, "the effort of self-objectification", of self-analysis, that he endlessly evokes?

Bourdieu, who summons intellectuals to collective action, warns that these attempts at mobilization should not be used "to serve struggles for leadership by an intellectual or a group of intellectuals" (p. 472). . . How can they trust him, when he is constantly and virulently preaching at them, and his works display an obsession, unmatched in the university field, with playing God? We can read what he says about "the desire to be God", in reference to Sartre: "an imaginary meeting of the *En-soi* and the *Pour-soi*", which ultimately may be only a transfigured version of the ambition to reconcile the satisfied plenitude of the bourgeois with the critical concern of the intellectual" (p. 297) — and transpose it here. "Carried away by his hegemonic dream", he seems not to see what he is doing and what he is saying. Upon careful reading, it is difficult to believe that sociological analysis "is one of the most powerful instruments of self-knowledge, as a social being, i.e., as a unique being".[8]

There is no need to waste time discussing, again, his tone; but we should emphasize the foreword, which starts with a scornful assessment of the university world ("hackneyed *topos* of the teaching profession's worship of the Book", "Heidegger-Hölderlinian revelations", p. 9) and, of course, with criticisms of School: the topics that he has just criticized "are inscribed in every mind that has been shaped by School" and they "always threaten to impede or mix up one's comprehension of the scientific analysis of books and reading" (p. 10). School definitely produces nothing but disastrous effects. . . So then, what does Bourdieu propose? That we should close the schools and replace them with a training in his methods and his view of the world, with his pedagogy(!)?

Pierre Bourdieu, who has so many titles and so much power, is wrong to want to import and impose his whims, his contempt and his self-complacency, his bellicose accents, into the intellectual field, the field of social sciences. This may be a battlefield, but not with whatever weapon you can find! Modern societies are striving to eliminate certain forms of weapons from war, to vote on certain prohibitions; war cannot be perpetual, every war comes to a close with a peace, or at least an armistice. Bourdieu carries on, with any means possible, a permanent war. That is surely one of the aspects of his *œuvre* that risk dragging it down into oblivion when he is no longer present to carry on the fight.

After having apostrophized writers and readers, "not to

mention the philosophers, of greater or of lesser stature", who affirm the irreducibility of a work of art and seek to set limits on science (pp. 10-11), Bourdieu, as always, justifies and praises the virtues and the superiority of sociological analysis. "Scientific analysis, when it manages to make clear what renders an art work *necessary*, that is, its informative formula, the generative principle, the *raison d'être*, provides the artistic experience and the pleasure that accompanies it with its best justification, its richest food" (p. 14). The scientific analysis of the social conditions of the production and the reception of a work of art "intensify the literary experience" *(ibid)*. [How, then, are we to read Shakespeare?]

Reminders as to what scientific analysis helps us to understand appear with a great frequency. The sociologist, who "in this sense is close to the philosopher according to Plato, is opposed to 'the friend of beautiful spectacles and beautiful voices', including the writer: the 'reality' that he is after cannot be reduced to the immediate sensory information to which it abandons itself; he is not looking to give a vision or a feeling, but to construct systems of intelligible relations that can give meaning to the sensory information" (p. 13). "Only an analysis of the genesis of the literary field in which the Flaubertian tale was developed can lead to a true comprehension of both the generative formula that formed the basis of the work of art and of the work by which Flaubert managed to produce it, at once objectifying both the generative structure and the social structure of which he is the product" (pp. 75-76). "Sociological analysis enables us to describe and understand the specific effort that the writer had to achieve, against these [social] determinations and at the same time thanks to them, in order to occur as a creator, i.e. as the *subject* of his own creation" (p. 153). What poor readers we would be without Bourdieu's scientific sociology!

> Why do these repeated assertions of the virtues of sociological analysis, which should wear me down, make me laugh instead? I have found the answer: they remind me of Aragon's reflection on *The Communists*. "What would we be without the party? Idiots like all the others. . . [who see] no further than the end of their noses. . .[9] Without Pierre Bourdieu, we would be idiots like the others. . . Pierre Bourdieu, like the Stalinist party, wants to educate, to convince, to win. Or to stigmatize, to exclude.

Criticizing internal interpretations of cultural works (formal, founded on the absolutization of the text) and external explanations as well (calling upon principles external to the *œuvre* such as social or economic factors. . .),[10] and wanting to break off radically with ordinary representations of the social world, Bourdieu invites us to try, "like all of modern science", the relational mode of thought". He explained that "thinking in terms of the field is *thinking relation-*

ally"; this time he refers to Cassirer, Tynianov, Kurt Lewin, Norbert Elias, Edward Sapir, Jakobson, Dumézil, Lévi-Strauss. . . "If I twisted Hegel's famous formula, I could say that *reality is relational:* what exists in the social world is relations" — not interactions or intersubjective bonds between agents, but objective relations that exist 'independently of the individual consciousness and wills', as Marx said".[11]

> The field is the fundamental concept of the science of cultural works, a concept that he redefines at considerable length once again. The field is a network of objective relations between various positions that control, that engender struggles of competition and of classification, establishing and altering the boundaries of the field and therefore of the hierarchies (p. 313, p. 324). Based on this definition, to which he adds ten more pages of finishing touches (fighting, battle, exclusion, social discrimination, domination, antagonism, etc.), Bourdieu states that "each of the positions has corresponding homologous viewpoints, [expressed through] literary and artistic works, of course, but also political acts and speeches, demonstrations or polemics, etc." (p. 322). The positions — "which one can and must treat as 'systems'" are "the products and the stakes of an ongoing conflict. In other words, the generating and unifying principle of this 'system' is the conflict itself" (p. 323).

The object of the science of the work of art is thus the relation between "the structure of the objective relations between the positions in the field of production (and between the producers who occupy those positions) and the structure of the objective relations between the positions [i.e., stands, or viewpoints] taken in the space of the works" (p. 325). It is characteristic of this science "to comprehend the social genesis of the literary field, the belief which supports it, the wordplay that goes on there, the interests and the material or symbolic rewards that may be found there. Quite simply, to look at things squarely and see them for what they are" (pp. 14-15).

Seeing things for what they are: this phrase is echoed relentlessly in descriptions of Pierre Bourdieu's imaginary world. And he ends the book by contrasting the literary text with science. "Science tries to state things as they are, without euphemism, and asks to be taken seriously even when it analyzes the bases of that completely unique form of *illusio* which is the scientific *illusio*" *(p. 458)*. The *illusio* makes a rather late appearance in Bourdieu's work, and it replaces the concept of interest picked up from Weber, who used the economic model to "discover the specific interests of the principal protagonists of the religious game". The *illusio* is "the fact of being invested, of being caught up in the game and by the game".[12] This shift indicates that Bourdieu rejects the charge of economism.

The literary field, and the scientific field, are fields like the others; like every field, they have their "dominant and their dominated segments, their conservatives and their avant-garde, their subversive fights and their mechanisms of reproduction", but the relations of power that lie at the basis take on "a special coloring". They have as a principle "a very particular type of capital": symbolic capital. The struggles, the interests, the strategies that one observes at play there cannot be reduced to those that "take place in the political field in ordinary existence".[13] Every field causes and calls forth a specific *illusio*. "The methodical transfer of problems and general concepts, specified each time by their very application, rests on the hypothesis that structural and functional homologies exist between all fields" (p. 256). Here, we begin to see the idea of a general theory of fields, only partly elaborated, he says, stressing that it has nothing to do with a transfer from the economic mode of thought, "contrary to appearances". "As I expect one day to be able to demonstrate, there is every reason to suppose that, far from being the fundamental model, the theory of the economic field is probably a particular case of the general theory of fields that is being built little by little, by a kind of empirically validated theoretical induction and which. . . constrains us to reconsider the assumptions of economic theory, especially in light of what we have casually learned from the analysis of the fields of cultural production" (pp. 257-258).

One of the major challenges in the conflict is the definition of the boundaries of the field, the definition of the legitimate practice. Bourdieu pauses over the dues that must be paid by any new entrant into the field, dues that consists primarily in "acquiring a specific code of conduct and expression", with entry leading the agent to discover "an ensemble of probable constraints", "the counterpart of a finite ensemble of objective potentialities" (p. 327); on this last point, one would like to see some examples. It is understandable that certain writers, readers, etc., would like to set limits on any "science" that is as reductive as that of Bourdieu: for him, creators espouse a finite ensemble of potentialities; for there to be any revolutionary audacity, "it would have to exist in a potential state within the system of the possible that is already realized, as *structural lacunae* that appear to expect and call for fulfillment. . . " (p. 327). Of course, it is understood that the call of "the structural lacunae of a system of the possible" is "never heard by any but those who . . . are sufficiently free with regard to the constraints inherent in the structure to be able to recognize as being for them a virtuality which, in a sense, exists only for them" (p. 332) (!). Here again, since you have read much of Bourdieu, you can continue on your own, explaining that it is their *habitus* and their position, and the relation between the two, that makes them free, etc.. Bourdieu calls it critical science; it is actually a line of thought that combines determinism, finalism, and tautology. The big chapter entitled "the author's point of view" (pp. 298-390) shows how the machine for producing statements functions, hopelessly going in circles.

Bourdieu assigns himself the task of bringing forth the literary field, and of making it autonomous, a long process whose beginning cannot be pegged to a specific date. Although he says he takes "delight" in reading works where the theory is "everywhere and nowhere" (p. 250), he separates his book into two quite unequal portions: theoretical considerations and empirical study. The latter section is written the way people talk: you won't recognize anything of Bourdieu. He proposes to provide a description of a specific state of the literary field, roughly speaking that which was constituted under the Second Empire, the heroic period, and then to offer a model of the state of the literary field "that was established in the 1880's" (p. 165). These pages must not be very "scientific" since, in reference to the proposal of a model, he writes: "In fact, only a solidly constructed chronicle could give the concrete feeling that this seemingly anarchistic and willingly libertarian universe. . . is the locus of a kind of well-regulated ballet wherein the individuals and the groups trace their paths . . . " (p. 165).

Bourdieu tells how the literary field is constituted, and

in fragments, remarks on the constitution of the artistic field. As a backdrop: "The long desolation of the Second Empire", (p. 91), the empress, the court, princess Mathilde, a sort of patron, and the salons. In the field, one finds a host of forgotten writers, and Baudelaire and Flaubert, the latter having contributed much to the constitution of the literary field. "Recreating Flaubert's point of view, that is, the point in social space from which his vision of the world was formed, and the social space itself, means giving [ourselves] the real possibility of sitting at the origin of a world the operation of which has become so familiar to us that we are no longer conscious of its regularities and the rules that it obeys" (p. 76). Bourdieu's reading of *A Sentimental Education* in order to oblige us "to consider the particular social conditions that lie at the origin of Flaubert's special clarity, and also the limits of that clarity". I should point out what has already been cited, that only an analysis of the genesis of the literary field in which Flaubert's tale was constituted "can lead to a real comprehension of both the generative formula that forms the basis of the work of art and of the work by which Flaubert managed to *produce it*. . . " (p. 75).

To show how the field was transformed at the end of the 19th century, Bourdieu summarizes his knowledge as if he were writing a textbook; for example, he lists like a schoolboy the names of the schools undergoing revolutions in poetry at the beginning of the century: "synthetism, integralism, impulsionism, aristocratism, unanimism, sincerism, subjectivism, druidism, futurism, intensism, floralism, simultaneism, dynamism, effreneism, totalism, etc.", all accompanied by the names of the poets (pp. 179-180), without actually giving the impression that he has a thorough, or even approximate, knowledge of all these movements, and without helping us to see the (scientific) interest of this enumeration. Have the incessant battles in poetry, hidden behind these words, really been shown and do they show the process of purification of poetry? Similarly, was it necessary, in the interest of achieving autonomy, to mention so many "pulp" novels, so many forgotten writers? Obviously, Bourdieu would say, it was necessary, and he seems to be very sure of the exactitude and the scientific quality of his description.

How can we prove that this list is not simply arbitrary? "The analyst who knows of the past only those authors that literary history has recognized as worthy of being preserved is dedicated to an intrinsically vicious form of comprehension and explanation: he can only reflect, without realizing it, the effects exerted by those authors whom he ignores . . . on the authors that he claims to interpret. . . He thereby keeps himself from really understanding all that which, in the very works of the survivors, as in their rejection, is the indirect product of the existence and the action of the authors who have disappeared" (pp. 106-107). There was a time when schools (secondary education and the Sorbonne) still talked about forgotten authors, giving their names along with brief and severe judgments, very seldom presenting any of their works. What leaves me perplexed by Bourdieu's claim of originality in his attempt to construct the literary field scientifically is that he produces something that resembles a traditional literary history, from school, in a form that sometimes has been considered outdated and not very likely to produce a higher understanding since it was always written second- (or third-) hand.

Certainly, there is a latent discussion, which will never be completed, going on today between those who stay with the great works and those who, making the effort to take an exceptionally broad view, also "make a detour past these so-called secondary works": Paul Bénichou, for example (who is never cited by Bourdieu), but who has sought out, read, and analyzed on his own these forgotten authors.[14] Bourdieu has not made any such effort; he has merely produced what seems to be a disorganized compilation that leaves the reticent reader on the field that he has thus reconstituted. This is one of the weak points of his theory: it is always based on insufficient and disparate materials. He talks about a method that requires "enormous work", which would be obvious if we really must explore the continent of forgotten works. But in reading him, one does not see any innovation, any "discoveries" in the field of producers, and even less in that of the consumers and their relations.

Bourdieu says his writings are "victims" (!) of "selective blindness".[15] But he is not reproached for his results, only for the nearly nil results relating to his announced ambitions. The inflated lists of proper names is not enough, for example, to show the effects that forgotten literature may have produced on those authors worthy of being preserved. As for the battle that constitutes the field, are there discoveries to be made between the pole of "pure art" (Flaubert) and the commercial pole (pulp fiction and industrial art), etc.? Bourdieu finds that literary people do not know how to read their authors, but one wonders sometimes what he means. His references at the bottom of the page and his index of names leaves one skeptical, because his sources are so restricted and so often out of date.

It is hard for the reader to conceive how one can pass from this grade-school literary history to all that Bourdieu says must be done. For example: "A genetic sociology *should also* incorporate in its model the action of the producers themselves, their claim of the right to be the sole judges of pictorial production, to produce themselves the criteria of perception and appreciation of their products; *it should* take into account the effect that might be exerted on them and on the image that they have of themselves and of their production, and, thereby, on their production itself, the image of themselves and of their production that the other agents engaged in the field reflect back to them: the other artists, and also the critics, the customers, the patrons, collectors, etc. . . the history of the specific institutions that are essential to artistic production *should be* paralleled by a history of the institutions that are essential to consumption. . . (p. 403) [emphasis by J.V.-L.].

Without pausing to take a breath, the book turns to the declaration of gigantic and unfeasible goals, so unfeasible that the author talks about them without trying to fulfill them. Better yet, sketching an outline of the elements one should know in order to understand the poetry of 1880 (p. 330), he concludes: "It would be completely unjust and useless to try to dismiss this requirement of reconstitution on the grounds that it is difficult to realize, practically speaking (which is not in doubt). In certain cases, scientific progress may consist in determining the assumptions and the *petitio principii* that implicitly engage the irreproachable (because unreflective) efforts of 'normal science' and in proposing research projects that would attempt to solve the questions that ordinary research holds as having been solved, simply for want of having posed them" (p. 331). It seems that Bourdieu would have trouble presenting, here, an indisputable example of what he is proposing.[16] Reading, rereading or skimming through this book, we see that in the end Bourdieu sticks to proposing programs which, if they were carried out, should prove the excellence of his views; this concept of the grand program belongs to a past era and testifies to a positivist and, one might say, rigid vision of research.

> The book, in spite of its volume and all its perambulations, comes up short: the postscript, "For a Corporatism of the Universal", shifts in register. It sets out to be "a normative standpoint founded on the conviction that it is possible to derive from the knowledge of the logic of the operation of the fields of cultural production a realistic program for a collective action on the part of the intellectuals" (p. 461). This chapter seems not to follow but to flee the preceding material; it seems to result from a dissatisfaction born of the confrontation between an unfinished (unfeasible) task and an unbounded ambition. There too, how many things would one have to analyze to see everything that threatens the autonomy of artists, writers and scholars, in these "times of restoration".

Countering the myth of the "natural-born intellectual" and the myth of the "Mandarin in his ivory tower", Bourdieu invites intellectuals to work collectively in the defense of their own interests, "to engage in a rational action in defense of the economic and social conditions of the autonomy of these privileged social universes where the material and intellectual instruments of what we call Reason are produced and reproduced" (p. 472). [Economic conditions, did we read? . . . Does he mean to say that we should take more money from the dominated in order to support a culture that, as readers of Bourdieu's earlier works, we know is arbitrary and that legitimates and reinforces the domination?] What intellectuals would be ready to join him, when he continually discredits and condemns them?

His proclamations seem to contradict his earlier writings, especially his defense of culture. "Here, I address myself to all those who conceive of culture not as a patrimony, a dead culture. . . nor as an instrument of domination and distinction, . . . but as an instrument of freedom that presupposes freedom, as a *modus operandi* allowing us to permanently get beyond the *opus operatum*, culture as an inert thing, and closed. They will grant me, I hope, the right that I grant myself to invite them to this modern incarnation of the critical power of intellectuals that could become a collective intellectual able to make its voice heard, singing the song of freedom, not recognizing any other limits but the constraints and controls that each artist, each writer and each scientist, armed with all the achievements of his predecessors, brings to bear upon himself and on all the others" (pp. 461-462).

This sentence is amazing: how is it that all "the

achievements of his predecessors" are so little recognized, so little used in his works in sociology — a science of which he seems to be the only founder, the only generator? And in the field of social sciences, however odd, however well or poorly constituted it may be (you might like to reread what he says about the dues to be paid), what constraints and controls ever impinged on his "science"?

Bourdieu sees intellectuals as benighted, and for twenty years he has wanted to set them free. But what makes him think that they would have allowed themselves to be so deceived? Has he had any response to his call? Is the scientist, in the final analysis, naive?

Footnotes

1. Pierre Bourdieu, *Raisons pratiques*. "Sur la théorie de l'action", Paris, le Seuil, 1994, p. 9.
2. Bourdieu generally omitted to indicate when these articles were first published, except for those which are co-authored. So many pages have already been read that the book seems more like a heterogeneous collection that a book in itself.
3. *L'Amour de l'art* (1969) concludes, " . . . the sacralization of culture and art, the 'currency of the absolute' adored by a society enslaved to the absolute of currency, fulfills a vital function while contributing to the consecration of the social order: for the men of culture to believe in barbarity and to persuade their barbarians within of their own barbarity, it is necessary and it is enough for them to be dissimulated and to dissimulate the social conditions that make possible not only that culture as second nature where society recognizes human excellence and which is experienced as a privilege of birth, but still legitimate (or, if you prefer, legitimatized) domination of a definition particular to the culture (p. 165).
   Les Règles de l'art (1992): "Here, I am addressing myself to all those who conceive the culture not as a patrimony, a dead culture to which one renders the obligatory worship of a pious ritual, nor as an instrument of domination and distinction, culture as a bastion and a Bastille, contrasted to the Barbarians inside and outside, often the same ones today, for the new defenders of the West, but as an instrument of freedom that presupposes freedom, as a *modus operandi* allowing one permanently to get beyond the *opus operatum*, culture as a thing, a closed concept (p. 462).
4. The Chapter "La genèse sociale de l'œil *(The social genesis of the 'eye')"* (based on the book by Michael Baxandall, *The Eye of the Quattrocento*), the chapter "A theory in the act of reading" (remarks on *A Rose for Emily*, by Faulkner) do not fit well into large book. One has to wonder whether Bourdieu read it again *da capo*, and whether he directs research that is intended to apply his method, in all its details. . . When he begins again, starting on page 11, his "resistance to analysis" (in italics), perhaps it is because he has the feeling that this book will not stand up very well to discussion?
5. What do we learn, for example, from his remarks on the so-

cial ageing of perfumes from Carven (pp. 354-355) or on the word games in *Libération* (p. 344)? Or from so many other incidental comments for which one does not see the need: "Lugné Poe, whose father spent his entire career in the bank" (p. 174), or the comparisons that one would like to ask him to justify: "Princess Mathilde's salon is the paradigm of these *bastard institutions*, the equivalent of which can be found in the most tyrannical regimes (fascist or Stalinist, for example)" (p. 80). Bourdieu does not seem to have reflected much on Stalinist Communism or on Fascism, this comparison is so far from being relevant.

6. This whole passage on *the dissymmetrical relation* that he takes it upon himself to establish . . . etc., copies (for laughs) one of Bourdieu's notes on Sartre. We've already seen Bourdieu's analysis of Sartre, the total intellectual, but this appendix "the total intellectual and the illusion of the absolute power of thought", pp. 293-297, deserves to be read and even re-read. It describes Pierre Bourdieu very well — "a privileged pariah, dedicated to cursing the (blessed) consciousness that prevents his happy coincidence with himself, and of the freedom that holds him remote from his condition and his conditionings. The malaise that he expresses is his discomfort at being an intellectual and not his discomfort in the intellectual world, where he is, in the final analysis, like a fish in water" (p. 297).
7. In his pages, Bourdieu attacks; in the footnotes, he often merely takes care to dissociate himself from others; the authors whom he names are surely not pharisees, or blind men; simply, he makes a point of reminding us that he is unique. For example: "When, in order to make my meaning more clear, I speak of *framing*, I risk evoking in the reader's mind the Goffmanian concept of *frame*, an ahistoric concept, from which I mean to dissociate myself (p. 329, N 29).
8. *Raisons pratiques, op. cit.*, p. 11.
9. Aragon, *Les Communistes*, Paris, La Bibliothèque française, t. II, 1951, p. 340.
10. On the criticism of internal interpretations and external explanations of cultural works, see in particular pp. 271-288. Bourdieu reprises the criticisms stated in "Pour une science des œuvres" (1986), published in 1994 (*Raisons pratiques, op. cit.,* pp. 62-68). What good are his critiques of analyses of

Marxist inspiration when he offers them in such a reductive way? "The success of the Impressionist revolution probably would not have been possible without the appearance of a group of young artists (painters) and young writers who were shaped by the 'overproduction' of graduates that came about due to the concomitant transformations of the school system" (*ibid*, p. 72).

11. Pierre Bourdieu, with Loïc J. D. Wacquant, *Réponses. Pour une anthropologie réflexive*, Paris, le Seuil, 1992, p. 72.
12. *Ibid*, p. 92.
13. Pierre Bourdieu, "Le champ intellectuel: un monde à part (The Intellectual field: A world apart)" in *Choses dites,* Paris, Editions de Minuit, 1987, pp. 167-169.
14. Among all the praises which José-Luis Diaz offers for Paul Bénichou's exceptional *œuvre*, he emphasizes the importance of Bénichou's work in rediscovering forgotten second-tier literary works. "To resist the insidious form of amnesia that comes from reducing art history to the masterpieces alone, Paul Bénichou made himself the untiring cicerone of the halls of literature and of thought, from the end of the Enlightenment and the first half of the 19th century." He explains how this delver into details knew "how to handle the telescope" and how his transverse investigations were fertile ("L'écrivain dans l'Histoire [The writer in History])", in "*Mélanges sur l'œuvre de Paul Bénichou,*" Paris, Gallimard, 1995, p. 60.)
15. "Le champ intellectuel : un monde à part", op. cit., p. 170.
16. Generally, the abandonment of an implicit hypothesis is justified by the (unplanned) working out of a solution to a problem that had been insoluble, and by the new facts that are thus explained. Thus what makes Planck's hypothesis on quantum theory, which indeed met opposition, so important is that it solved completely the problem of radiation from black bodies. Cf. Emilio Segrè, *Les Physiciens modernes et leurs découvertes* Paris, Fayard, 1984, pp. 101-107.

Chapter VII

"Thinking Outside Of Bourdieu"

An Invitation to Reflexive Anthropology (1992)

Introducing the collection of seminars that Pierre Bourdieu gave in Chicago and Paris in 1987, Wacquant affirmed the importance of his work, calling it "one of the most imaginative and most fertile corpora of sociological theory and research in the post-war era (p. 13) and defined what is special about his pedagogy. "In order to escape the intellectualist bias inherent in the school approach to education, and in accordance with his anti-intellectualist philosophy of practice, Bourdieu relies on practical comprehension to gradually introduce principles of sociological reason for discursive mastery. He defends and produces a complete and self-referential pedagogy that rejects the partition of theoretical and empirical operations into isolated activities and distinct territories. . ." (p. 10).

The book offers to have us follow his *modus operandi*, his

"mind in action" (p. 7). Bourdieu repeats the same thing he says throughout his research: "What is most important is not so much the results themselves as the process by which they are obtained" (p. 56). In short, this book is a guide to reading, an apologist's summary of the work, and the writer of the preface says that "this reflexive sociology cannot, under penalty of self-destruction, require a closed mind" (p. 10). Why write something so obvious? What body of thought would say: I am in favor of closing myself in on myself? And the preface-writer, apparently too reverential to be sincere, adds: "An invitation to think with Bourdieu is an invitation to think beyond Bourdieu and against him, any time it may be necessary" (p. 10). Just try to think against him. You will be labeled immediately: "blind", "malicious", "Pharisaic", even "clown"...

The collection is interesting not so much for the definitions and what Bourdieu has to say about the theoretical functions of the concepts that are central to his work, as for the amount of space allocated to certain obsessive ideas his writings. First of all, of course, he deplores the faulty way his works have been read: "The theoretical implications, the anthropological bases — the theory of practice, the philosophy of action, etc. — of my research have gone almost completely unnoticed in France. Instead, there have been very scholastic discussions. . . . But the main thing is, I believe, that only political *theses* were seen — on the school system and on culture in particular — in what I saw as an attempt to build a general anthropology founded on a historical analysis of the specific characteristics of contemporary societies" (p. 134).

Complaining about the poor reception of his work in France, Bourdieu also complains about faulty readings in English. In his assessment of *Homo Academicus*, in *Sociology*, Richard Jenkins criticized the sociologist's complicated style. Bourdieu could not accept it: "When he gets to the point of reproaching me for an expression like 'the doxic modality of discourses', he betrays not only his ignorance ('doxic modality' is Husserl's expression . . .) but above all his ignorance of his ignorance and the social conditions that make it possible" (p. 144). One might remind Bourdieu that he calls himself a sociologist and not a philosopher, and that, even without being incompetent ignoramuses, sociologists may not have read Husserl. It should also be said that his criticisms of his critics appear comical in their breadth, their diversity and their tone. Mr. Jenkins did not cast "a reflexive view" on his critique, and for that reason he failed to perceive the "anti-intellectualist dispositions"[1] hidden under his praise of simplicity, his polemical objectivations are false, he did not consider whether his worship of the "plain" might be associated with his academic tradition, etc.; in short, he did not understand the true intention of the work, he did not consider the "*arbitrary aspects of the stylistic traditions* imposed and inculcated by the different systems of instruction", and the forms of *censure* imposed by the requirements of the English universities (p. 144). Ouch! That is about all that Bourdieu has to say to this rascal who took on against his scholarship.[2]

> As Bourdieu sees it, he has every reason to be in a bad humor, for he starts off his writings, or disperses throughout them, all sorts of recommendations and explanations to forestall any possible misunderstanding, and he even adds recommendations against the probable use of practical recommendations . . . (p. 158).

After he kills off the misreadings, Bourdieu turns to another of his favorite topics, which is "disseminated" in the collection: the sociology of sociology "is the necessary precondition of every rigorous sociological practice" (p. 48). Another topic that is flogged to death: "Paraphrasing Kant, I could say that research without theory is blind and that theory without research is empty" (p. 137). Wacquant, who in the introduction spoke of one of "the most imaginative and most fertile corpora of sociological theory and research in the post-war era", questions him on the place theory holds in his work. He wants to "point out an enigma": "You are often presented and read as a 'social theorist' . . . However, I am struck by the scarcity of purely theoretical propositions in your work" (p. 133). [No point in our dwelling too long on the excessive space devoted to "purely theoretical propositions" not only in *Outline of A Theory of Practice* and in *The Logic of Practice*, but in *Reproduction*, *Distinction*, *The Rules of Art*, etc..] Bourdieu must read of his own works very cursory, for he answers: "I don't much like theory that exhibits itself, that puts itself on parade, theory that is made for show. . . . For me, theoretical reflection is manifest only when it is dissimulated in the scientific practice which it informs" (pp. 134-135). Is Wacquant surprised? — he interjects, "But you cannot deny that there is theory in your work or, to be more precise, an ensemble of 'instruments of thought' . . . of very general applicability?" Bourdieu answers: "Certainly, but these tools are visible only in the results which they produce . . ." "The thread that connects one part of my research to the next is a logic that is inseparably both empirical and theoretical" (p. 135). In short, his theory is not a "theorist" theory, it is "presented in the form of a program of perception and action, a scientific *habitus* . . . , which is revealed only in the empirical work in which it is put into action" (p. 136). You must know — let us hope — the state of sociology: "Unfortunately, the socially dominant model of sociology still rests today on an entrenched distinction and a practical divorce between empirical research without theory. . . and the pure theorists' theory with no object. . ." (p. 137).

This brings us to another constant of Bourdieu's output: an emphasis on the importance and the demands of his work, and an explanation of the difficulties, the hazards that he avoids, the challenges that he makes, the risks he takes, "the errors" that he acknowledges (?), his hesitations. . . , etc.. "At every moment, I would like to be able to see that which I am not seeing, and I always ask myself, somewhat obsessively, which box have I not opened, what is the overlooked parameter that still influences me?" (p. 183). If Bourdieu experiences, as any researcher does, anxiety at every stage of his work, it is hard to understand why he does not tolerate criticism but challenges his critics in advance; he should read them, and perhaps he would see that he has indeed overlooked one parameter, which continues to influence him. . .

Saying that the situation of the sociologist is "quasi-desperate", that "the epistemological rift is often a social rift", he declares: "Practicing radical doubt in sociology is a little like setting oneself outside the law" (p. 211). The results that Bourdieu publishes, defending them against every critic, and his tireless assertion of their absolutely scientific nature, leaves the reader skeptical about whether he practices what he calls radical doubt. He claims to have a classically scientific practice. "The social sciences are subject to the same rules that apply to the other sciences: one must produce coherent explanatory systems, hypotheses and propositions organized into parsimonious models that can account for a vast number of empirically observable facts and that are liable to being refuted by more powerful models, obeying the same conditions of logical coherence, systematicity and empirical refutability. When I talk with my friends who are chemists, physicists or neurobiologists, I am struck by the similarities between their practice and mine. A typical day for a sociologist, with his experimental groping, his statistical analyses, his readings of specialized articles and his discussions with colleagues, closely resembles that of an ordinary scientist" (p. 159).

Here, Bourdieu repeats what he had said at length in *In Other Words: Essays Towards a Reflexive Sociology* [*Choses Dites*] (1987): "For me, intellectual life is closer to the life of an artist than to the routines of academic existence", and he describes his life: ". . . the pleasure of those interviews which, starting at ten in the morning, go on all day; and the extreme diversity of a job where one might, in the same week, interview a business leader and a bishop, analyze a series of statistical tables, consult historical documents, observe a conversation at a bar, read theoretical articles, talk with other researchers, etc.. I would not at all have liked to go and punch a time clock at the National Library every day".[3]

Notice the scientist's "objective outlook": the "routines of academic existence", punching a time clock at the library; he uses such phrases to caricature the work of other researchers, probably in part because he has no idea what it is like to spend a day reading at the national library. There are, of course, books that can only be found there; acquired knowledge, i.e. mastering all the tools that the library provides, allows speed, inventiveness, and the bouncing around of ideas; one never goes to the library with one's ideas fully formed, and it is too bad that Bourdieu has never spent a whole day there! Let's drop this "lesson" right here, merely noting that it is strange

> that his books are presented as enormous philosophizing essays: he assures us that he is engaged in an abundance of activities, but he gives the impression of spending all his time writing about and re-hashing his own theory.

Sociology is a science, and even, says Bourdieu, "a science that is far more advanced than its critics, including those among sociologists themselves, are willing to recognize" (p. 151); and he repeats: "Sociology is a relatively advanced science, much more so than is generally believed among sociologists" (p. 194). But he also talks about the difficulty that this science has in "*affirming* its scientific quality, that is, attaining it and having it be recognized" (p. 159). In his introduction, Wacquant made much of the characteristics of this science: "Science is indeed, as Gramsci observed, an eminently political activity", but it cannot be reduced to a politics (p. 38). "For Bourdieu, sociology is an *eminently political* science"; it cannot be "neutral, detached, apolitical" (p. 40). "The more scientific sociology becomes, and the more politically pertinent and efficient it becomes, even if only as an instrument of criticism, as a system of defense against the forms of symbolic domination that prevent us from becoming true political agents" (p. 41). Bourdieu himself affirms: "It is an ethics because it is a science. If what I say is true, if it is true that it is through knowledge of the determinations procured by science that a form of freedom becomes possible which is the condition and the correlation of an ethics, then it is also true that a reflexive science of society implies or includes an ethics. . ." (p. 171).

These propositions, which exploit the positive reception that our usual understanding grants to the nouns "science" and "scientist", must be examined and treated on a hierarchical basis. First, we have to ask whether all forms of intellectual research are science. If so, sociology has no more scientific merit than another; if the contrary case is true, we would have to specify what is a science and show what sociology has achieved (rather than by traditional philology, for example) to support its claim to being scientific. In the second place, one must consider the proposition: "physics and biology are political activities", not that physics, or biology, do not have profound political consequences — and at various levels, which is obvious — but is the practice of a physicist or a biologist a political practice? Bear in mind that Bourdieu often says that pure sciences, like mathematics or physics, are "universes purified of everything that causes problems, like sexuality or politics".[4]

By the same token, does the proposition "physics (or biology), because it is a science, is an ethics" make sense other than marginally? (— the constraints imposed on scientific thought have an ethical dimension.) Or subjectively? (— my personal way of giving an ethical dimension to my presence on earth and to advance physics or biology). Bourdieu, so prompt to stigmatize (others) for the lack of intellectual rigor and its malignant intentionality (the error is not innocent. . .) does not ask himself these questions. Aren't premises that are so poorly defined actually an intellectual shell game?

To go further: isn't the claim of a scientific activity that is "eminently political" in conflict with the specialization that is essential to the scientific practice? One's thoughts may turn to the time when Pasteur discovered the origin of rabies *and* the remedy for rabies, one might cite Fermi and Wigner, eminent quantum physicists (and émigré antifascists) who fifty years ago contributed their engineering talents to the *Manhattan Project.* Nevertheless it should be noted, even as we deplore it, that the very movement of science separates, in both the actors and in time, the development of knowledge and its validation, on the one hand, and its implementation, on the other hand. Keynes' theory, elaborated in the 1930's, picked up and reformulated by economists with government ties, only took on its full political significance and its recognition until after 1945. Bourdieu cannot be unaware of that, so then what do his claims mean?

Another little prejudice: that political orientation and scientific development are mutually reinforcing, the conjunction making them "relevant and efficient". Nowadays, these activities are rather more separate than joined together; and we certainly have had, in recent history, examples that were scientifically as well as politically disastrous, of the degradation of science by the political. Perhaps the experiment with Lysenko-ism, for example, deserves some reflection, especially as regards social science, especially on the part of an intellectual who was educated in the heated Stalinist atmosphere of the ENS in the 1950's. Even if abandoning an immature radicalism is a sign of disenchantment, the unspoken beliefs that support the absolute positivity granted to science, supposed to be unconditionally tied to progress, and thus to anyone who is a practitioner, should be "objectified". Already in 1901, when Taine's star was fading, Leon Blum noted: "There is an illusion and a kind of fetishism inherent in our docile expectation that science will bring about the renewal of society".[5]

Wacquant's question whether his "social consecration", i.e. his election to the College of France, had affected his scientific practice, and Bourdieu's answer both merit special attention. "I believe that, if I have some small chance of not being done in by the consecration, I owe it to having worked to analyze the consecration. I even think that I will be able to use the authority that this consecration has given me to lend more authority to my analysis (which I believe to be liberating) of the logic and the effects of the consecration" (p. 182).

> And what, then, are the results of his analysis of the effects of the consecration? Wacquant, responsible for annotating Bourdieu's remarks, refers readers to a few pages in *The State Nobility* (1989).
>
> The first text he indicates (2nd part, Chapter 2, "The Rites of the Institution", pp. 140-162) talks about competitive entrance to the "elite schools". The second text (the first pages of the 5th part, "The Power of the State and Power Over the State", pp. 533-539) repeats his old analyses on the contribution of the school institution to the preservation of the social order and the violent reactions that this analysis supposedly invoked. "The ruses of bad social faith are impenetrable", wrote Bourdieu (p. 534, N 2). The title of professor at the College of France is indubitably an academic title like any other. What is an academic title? "The academic title is a public and official attestation, granted by a collectively recognized authority, of competence in a sphere that can never be broken down and measured as to what extent and in what proportions it is technical or social, but which is still independent of subjective and prejudiced appreciations (that of the title-holder himself or his close relations, for example)" (p. 539). The academic institution is "one of the authorities through which the State exerts its monopoly on legitimate symbolic violence: by imposing the legitimate evaluation of each agent, through the act that consecrates him (like granting a diploma from the Ecole Polytechnique, the *agrégé* Pedagogical Honors certificate, etc.) or condemns him (as excluded from the class of degree-holders), the *school verdict* reconciles the agents, at least partially, and, without putting a defini-

> tive end to the war of all against all for the monopoly of the legitimate point of view, it institutes an eminent point of view, which all the others must take into account, even if only to contest it" (p. 539).

Pierre Bourdieu, so set on objectivation, has not produced — how strange! — an analysis of his campaign and his election to the College, his sometimes "ferocious fights" and the expulsions that were entailed. In what state was the scientific field after the battle?

What is a scientific field? "The scientific field, as a system of the objective relations between the positions acquired (in previous conflicts) is the place (i.e. the playing field) of a competitive struggle that has as a *specific* stake the monopoly of the *scientific authority* defined as the inseparable duality of technical capability and social power. . . . To say that the field is a battleground is not only to break with the irenic image of the 'scientific community'. . . It also means remembering that the very functioning of the scientific field *produces and supposes a specific form of interest*".[6] Bourdieu's only "scientific" statement on his consecration was when he said that the authority thus conferred had enabled him to give even greater authority to his analyses: this can be observed in the publication of his least "scientific" initiatives, *The Weight of the World, Free Exchange, On Television,* and *Acts of Resistance: Against the Tyranny of the Market* [*Contre-feux*]. His consecration enables him to publish whatever he feels like publishing.

On this question of consecration — and the terrorist and off-handed way he makes use of it — Bourdieu has forgotten to adopt *the reflexive point of view*... for adopting it means "to question the privilege of the knowing subject, who is arbitrarily freed, as a pure noetic, from the effort of objectivation" (pp. 184-185). Bourdieu transforms himself into a new Eliacin promoted to the College: "As for me — to answer precisely your question about what I do with my knowledge of the university world — I believe that my well-known clumsiness in university strategies attests that I am incapable of putting them to cynical use. . ." (p. 183). He had just distinguished two ways that sociological analyses could be used in the intellectual world: a clinical use, i.e. searching among the achievements of the science for "instruments of an unbiased self-comprehension", and a cynical use, searching for "instruments to aid one's 'success' in the social world . . . or to guide one's strategies in the intellectual world" (p. 182).

How was Bourdieu elected to the College? Was it by chance? Was it a miracle? Because he is maladroit and the opposite of cynical, he affirms. Or is it because he really is the best that this election was to some extent imposed on him? (Doesn't he say "what happened to me"?) (p. 182).

That Bourdieu speaks of his ingenuity, of his clumsiness, to a group of doctoral students in Chicago, is a want of rigor and of modesty. But for him to try to make us believe that, here in France, is a show of cynicism or complete blindness (unless this is an example of the "impenetrable ruses of bad faith". . .) It is understandable if he does not want to "show his hand" and expose the secrets of his career, his strategies, his battles, and his consecration, but he should stop thinking we are so credulous and stop presenting, for example, *Homo Academicus* as "an enterprise in self-awareness and an attempt to test the limits of reflexivity in the social sciences" (p. 184).

This contradiction between words and deeds casts a shadow on the benevolence that he wants to show the students in inviting them into "the intimacy of the workshop" (p. 191). The ideas here have been expounded a thousand times over: the deconstruction of the object, the capacity of rebuilding the object scientifically, the idea that "the zenith of art is being able to entertain the big so-called 'theoretical' questions about so-called 'empirical' objects that are very precise, and often quite minor, even somewhat ridiculous" (p. 191), and a necessary familiarity with "practical tasks as vulgarly banal as those which are part of the sociologist's job. . ."; "the sociologist is somebody who goes out in the street and questions whoever comes along, listening and trying to learn from him" (p. 176).

Does Bourdieu really practice the practical, banal tasks of the trade? Claude Grignon, analyzing his disillusions, identified the tendencies that led him to leave Bourdieu's group, and he described what seemed obvious to him upon reading *Distinction:* it was conceived on the model of "the philosophy essay for the entrance examination to the ENS or the *agrégé*, in the 1950's". Bourdieu, having promoted himself to being the only judge of "the internal coherence" of his personal theory, "had put on the back-burner" the exploitation of the research that was in progress, failed to take up any new projects, and had forsaken the empirical tasks of description and of observation, already twenty years ago.[7]

This view from a former follower — who had the wisdom to wait to find and explain the reasons for his great disappointment — consolidates what a reading of Bourdieu shows. His principles on the interview, exposed at the end of *The Weight of the World*, and the interviews that he conducted and published without recognizing how manipulative they were, show his ignorance of the practical tasks. Interviews are not part of his daily practice; as for the way he reads statistics, it has been shown more than once that he only uses them as a simple illustrations of his theory.

Of his seminars, it is worth retaining what he says of his interests as a reader of philosophy. "It is enough for me to open such and such recent (French) treatise on political philosophy to imagine what I might have said if my philosophical training had been my only intellectual equipment. I think, nevertheless, that it is absolutely determinant" (p. 133). He says, as I have quoted, that he reads and rereads philosophy every day, that he constantly works with philosophers, and he constantly gives the philosophers work to do. "Philosophical tools — this may be somewhat sacrilegious — are on exactly the same plane as mathematical tools: I do not see an ontological difference between one of Kant's or Plato's concepts and a factorial analysis. . ." (p. 133.)

> Bear in mind that factorial analysis is a technique proposed by psychologists to enable one to highlight the most significant elements of a table of statistics. It is not exactly a mathematical tool. Admittedly, evoking his youth as a student in the 1950's, he says: "I studied mathematics, and the history of the sciences",[8] but what kind of mathematics?

This assertion raises two questions. First, the knowledge, the familiarity, that a sociologist/philosopher would have of mathematical tools — this brings to mind the opinion that Bourdieu himself gave to two scientists, Alan Sokal and Jean Bricmont, who recently revealed the "intellectual impostures" committed by French specialists in social sciences who made a flawed or dishonest use of the tools of the exact sciences; that should be food for thought and should encourage the greatest prudence in the use of mathematical tools.[9] Second, doesn't going back to philosophy hurt or put to death sociology? Putting sociology to death: by according philosophy the determinant share of a sociologist's training, Bourdieu pretends not to realize that the vast majority of the researchers in his own "workshop", the students in his seminar, and no doubt those in Chicago, have no background in philosophy. To my knowledge, he never said to his students and to his researchers that they had any need for that aspect of culture.

Isn't this return to philosophy, as I have hypothesized in the introduction, the sociologist's painful and covert admission of his sociology's inability to explain the world and its miseries? Even if, on the contrary, explaining why he chose to go into sociology, on various occasions he stated his hope of success: "I think that, given what I was, socially, given what one might call my social conditions of production, sociology was the best thing I could do, if not to come to agree with life, at least to find the world in which I was condemned to live more or less acceptable. In this limited sense, I think that I have succeeded in my effort: I have conducted a kind of self-therapy which, I hope, has at the same time produced tools which can be of some utility for others" (p. 183). In the same vein, he had said a little earlier: "Of all the intellectual trades, the sociologist's trade is probably the one that that I could do most happily, in every sense of the expression — at least, I hope so."[10] Unless this return to philosophy is a sign of the uniqueness of his own role: there might be sociologists trained in sociology who "apply", and he himself, who "thinks", who theorizes, and therefore who absolutely needs his training in philosophy. Perhaps we should consider, here, one of Wacquant's ideas: "One of the signs by which we recognize a truly innovative, i.e. generative, mode of thought is not only its capacity to transcend the particular intellectual context and the particular empirical ground of its initial declaration to produce new propositions, but also its capacity to conceptualize itself, even to exceed itself in thought" (p. 10).(!) [Read that over again, take your time, to get the full measure of the Bourdieusian mode of thought.]

There are chapters devoted to the core concepts of his *oeuvre*; we might pause at the umpteenth presentation of the "field". The concept of the "field" is used in a strikingly fuzzy way, whereas Wacquant sees it as being used "in a very technical and precise way" (p. 71). Scientific field, literary field, artistic field, field of power, religious field, legal field, field of manufacturing, field of housing production, field of territorial powers, political field, economic field, journalistic field, field of ideological production, field of cultural production, field of painting, field of institutions of higher education, field of political science, field of political marketing, university field, field of prestigious schools, field of haute couture, field of the comic strip, field of pop art, field of publishing, field of contemporary physics, field of art galleries, for example, etc. (and let's not forget the sub-fields: the sub-field of limited production, the sub-field of mass production. . .). All of these crop up in Bourdieu's treatises. The field is a game, in which the players in various contests compete, playing their best cards (their species of capital) which vary according to the field, etc.. Interminable in his abstract "descriptions" — which appear very "true-to-life" but which are unverifiable — Bourdieu (in spite of his instructions on the necessary but "inter-connected" steps in the analysis of the field), avoids coming to grips with it, dragging it out with no possible terminus, no possible hiatus. "The social cosmos consists of all of these relatively autonomous social microcosms, spaces of objective relations which are the loci of a logic and a need that are specific and irreducible to those which govern other fields" (p. 73). How can one arrive at a global representation, a global explanation of French society? For Bourdieu, this is one of the fundamental concepts — along with *habitus* and capital — of his philosophy of action. It is an unusable concept or one that drags us into nominalism.

Changing the label of the concepts (interest, *illusio*, libido, etc.), the excessive wordplay, the quite impossible to determine volume of Bourdieu's intellectual interests, and the quite impossible to read volume of pages published, underscore the disproportion of intent;[11] Bourdieu wants to know absolutely everything, to hold everything in his hands, to explain everything. The very announcement of his project tends to show how impossible it is. The theoretician's demiurgic ambition leads to a loghorrea that shifts between the pathetically pessimistic and the comically banal, and harping on one string.

This collection of seminars mixes self-satisfaction with unfounded condemnations (who are "the historians" who "often condemn themselves to anachronism because of their use of ahistorical or de-historicized" concepts? etc., p. 70). That Bourdieu is unable, here as in his articles, to formulate a conclusion, or at least to offer in conclusion some powerful idea, makes clear the limitations of such an approach. The *last sentence* requires analysis: "The participating objectivation, which is surely the apex of the sociological art, is only realizable (to some extent) if it rests on as complete as possible an objectivation of the interest to objectify which is inherent in the fact of the participation; and on a suspension of this interest and the representations that it induces" (p.

231). Given this consideration, which so closely resembles so many of the preceding propositions, and which refers to a project that cannot be realized, one wonders why the author does not go on talking, repeating to us things that he has told us a hundred times before.

In this book, Bourdieu wanted to clarify the ethical and political implications of his work and to reflect on the social effects that he would wish to and that he may produce. How can one have such a positivist and such a simple-minded view of the effects of a work, of the impact it could have? Bourdieu should ponder a thought from Martial Guéroult, a philosopher whom he admired: "The greatest and most durable influences on things and on mankind have been exerted by works that were calmly contemplated by the intelligence . . . The meditation necessary to the workings of the intelligence, he distance, far from separating man from things, creates, on the contrary, one of the essential conditions for mastering them: one is less able to influence the course they take when one has plunged into their stream."[12]

Footnotes

1. Note that Jenkins's anti-intellectualist disposition is considered condemnable, but that speaking of Bourdieu's anti-intellectualist philosophy of the practice is positive.
2. Pierre Bourdieu, in the foreword of *Choses dites* (Paris, Editions de Minuit, 1987, p. 8) wrote that he was content to express orally, in "a real dialogue", "explanations, denials and refutations that scorn or dislike engendered by self-destructive simplifications due to incomprehension and incompetence or stupid or base charges made in bad faith" dissuaded him from formulating in writing, because of "the ellipses of academic arrogance and the reticence of scientific propriety". In this *written* foreword to *oral and published* and in some cases translated remarks, Bourdieu said that he was shocked by the "pharisaism" of some of the reproaches made against him. Among the reproaches that Bourdieu inspires in me, I would probably list first of all the brutal manners that he imposes in the university field: a "scientist", even the most dedicated, cannot go around saying that others, all or almost all the others, are malevolent, half-blind, pharisees, etc.
3. Bourdieu, "Fieldwork in philosophy" (translated from German), in *Choses dites, op. cit,* p. 38.
4. Pierre Bourdieu, "Une science qui derange", *Questions de sociologie*, Paris, Editions de Minuit, 1980, pp. 21-22. (This interview with Pierre Thuillier initially appeared in *La Recherche* under the title: "La sociologie est-elle une science?")
5. Leon Blum, *Nouvelles Conversations de Goethe avec Eckermann,* (1901), quoted by Christophe Charle, *Paris fin de siècle,* Paris, Le Seuil, 1998, p. 171.
6. Pierre Bourdieu, "Le champ scientifique", *Actes de la recherche en sciences sociales,* June 1976, Nos 2-3, p. 89.
7. Claude Grignon, "Le savant et le lettré, ou l'examen d'une désillusion", *Revue européenne des sciences sociales,* T XXXIV, 1996, No. 103. See pp. 83-85 in particular.
   In 1987, Bourdieu spoke about the "enthusiasm" that would create "cohesion" in the group that he was heading up (*Choses dites, op. cit.,* p. 38); it is hard to believe that he had forgotten the departures, the in-fighting in his group and all the disillusions about which Claude Grignon speaks.
8. *Choses dites, op. cit.,* p. 14.

9. Cf. Alan Sokal, Jean Bricmont, *Impostures intellectuelles,* Paris, Editions Odile Jacob, 1997.
10. *Choses dites, op. cit.,* p. 38.
11. I read more than 10,000 pages, over and over again, and I reiterate that I ended up with the feeling that there were very few things worth retaining.
12. Martial Guéroult, *Leçon inaugurale* at the Collège de France, December 4, 1951 (Chaire d'Histoire et technologie des systèmes philosophiques, p. 5.

Chapter VIII

OUTSPOKENNESS: BOURDIEU AND PÉCUCHET ON *FREE EXCHANGE* (1994)

In the early 1990's, Pierre Bourdieu "the scientist" and Hans Haacke the artist,[1] feeling themselves to be "in affinity", decided to tape and then edit a discussion in which "each one would add information and reflections, and react to the other' reactions".[2] Hoping to preserve "the spontaneity of the original exchange", they hoped even more that despite the political and cultural changes that had occurred in the United States and France (the interview took place at the end of 1991, and the editing work was completed at the end of 1993), this dialogue would preserve its "efficacy" [*efficacité*]. What does *efficacité* mean? According to the Petit Robert dictionary, it is the "Capacity to produce the maximum results with the minimum of effort and expenditure." Minimum of effort, I believe, but what are the results? And where is the science? For we must not forget the Inaugural Lesson that Bourdieu gave on April 23, 1982 at the College of France, using the words "science" and "scientist" more than seventy times, to show that he was engaging, scientifically, in a scientific sociology.

The "scientist" and the artist talk, and repeat themselves quite often, to expose and grapple with the forms of domination that are exerted in the worlds of art, literature, etc., to summon the intellectual creative people to a kind of resistance, to convince them "that it is possible to invent outrageous forms of symbolic action", to place all "the resources of literary and artistic imagination at the service of symbolic struggles against symbolic violence" (p. 29). Bourdieu relies, he says, on Hans Haacke's works, "symbolic machines that work like traps and make the public take action" (p. 29). He wants a countervailing power to develop, that would bring together teams of researchers, artists, theater people and publicity specialists, thus mobilizing "a force equivalent to the symbolic forces that we are up against" (p. 111).

> Two of the ten works by Hans Haacke that are exhibited and discussed in *Free Exchange* allow us to see what Bourdieu defines as "symbolic machines that work like traps, etc.."
>
> One work is entitled *Raise the Flag*, 1991. Hans Haacke comments: "The title of the work borrows the first sentence of a famous Nazi song, *Horst-Wessel-Lied.* On the flag

in the center, you can read: 'Roll call — German industry in Iraq". The image of a death's-head is a photograph of an SS emblem. The other flags present the viewer with a list of German companies" (p. 32). One of the companies named on the flag asked for an temporary injunction: Hans Haacke immediately called his source, a journalist at *Der Spiegel*. He answered: "It's remarkable. My article didn't get any response out of Ruhrgas whatsoever. But you did, you got it. Apparently, if it is in the public space, they react. It bothers them. It creates a sensation." "The result of the complaint", Haacke says, was that "an insert had to be slipped into the exhibition catalogue, explaining that it was not Ruhrgas itself but a subsidiary company . . . that had delivered the material in question to Iraq! Thus, out of the 21 companies lisyed on my flags, the name of Ruhrgas stood out" (p. 31).

A second example is the piece, "Freedom Will Now Be Sponsored, Out of Petty Cash", 1990. One of the watch towers on "the border of peace", i.e. the Berlin Wall, was used for this project. "Its windows were re-done with tinted windowpanes, like the *Palast Hotel* in East Berlin. . . And like the windows of West German police vehicles, wire mesh protected them from thrown rocks. On the roof, the searchlight was replaced with a slowly rotating Mercedes star emblem. . . for years, at the top of Europa Center, the tallest building in the heart of the fashionable shopping area in Western Berlin, a Mercedes star . . . used to turn." Inscriptions in bronze letters were placed on two opposite sides of the tower, drawn from a Daimler-Benz advertising series: a sentence from Shakespeare, "Readiness is all", and one from Goethe, "Art will always remain art". Haacke then described Daimler-Benz's activities in Hitler's accession to power (pp. 96-97). The work was burned down. Bourdieu asks him: "It was almost as if you had wanted to encourage people to burn the work — did you foresee that?" (p. 100). No, the artist

> answers, and he explains the public reactions to the work and to the fire: "I believe that most of the passersby in Graz did not respond to my work as a piece of art but only as a political statement. Consequently, the fire was also perceived exclusively as a political act. It is only in the city's cultural circles that it was also interpreted as an attack against art" (p. 101).

These rather long and rather tedious descriptions are apparently necessary to clarify the "outrageous" forms of symbolic action, "the very powerful symbolic weapons" that so fill Bourdieu with enthusiasm (p. 29). Here, he astonishes me: he has said to us that he read *A Sentimental Education* as nobody before him had read it; why, then, doesn't he consider the harsh remarks made there against the foolishness of political art? Why, when he has spoken about the blows he struck for freedom, at the time of "triumphant Stalinism", of the "exasperating" "Stalinist pressure" at the ENS in 1951,[3] does he not see that Hans Haacke conceives and executes his "art" in full affinity with standards worthy of Zhdanov? [I can see that I weaken my case by underlining something so obvious. For an American art critic who does not like Hans Haacke (and vice versa), speaking "about the Stalinist ethics that reigned more or less everywhere among the artists, and the critics" (p. 56), cited two works by Haacke...]

What does this dialogue offer, that looks to affirm the

independence of the intellectual and of the critical artist, that looks to invent the weapons for their defense? Bourdieu, always sarcastic in evoking the "circular circulation" of praise between a small number of producers,[4] by no means shies away from the "dual circulation" of eulogistic considerations. "What strikes me in your artistic approach is that your work as a critical artist is accompanied by a critical analysis of the art world and even of the conditions of artistic production . . . I have trouble finding equivalents in the history of art, literature and philosophy (one example comes to mind, Karl Kraus . . . You have an absolutely remarkable 'eye' to see the particular forms of domination that are exerted on the art world..." (p. 11). "Actions like yours are truly valuable, these days" (p. 87). "You are proof that a person who is practically alone can produce an immense impact by breaking up the game, by destroying the rules, and often by scandal, the quintessential instrument of symbolic action" (p. 89). "Another merit of what you do is. . . that you do not accept being condemned to esotericism as a *fait accompli*" (p. 110).

Is this mania for rendering judgment and making a point just one of Bourdieu's professorial tics? No, for Haacke too knows how to play that game very well. "Your books are translated and read everywhere, and they recently inspired a group of young artists in Germany" (p. 108).

"Would you be surprised if I said that your writing is effective? Through the game of writing you manage to communicate your scientific discoveries in an incredibly clear and sometimes almost familiar tone. Going from the more abstract to the more concrete, you put your finger on the most complex social realities, and you have rendered a formidable public service. You have taught me so much, and I have enjoyed it" (p. 112).

It is clear that they enjoy listening to themselves, but in the dialogue Bourdieu is often nothing but the foil for an artist who is very, very satisfied with himself. An art critic judged that two of his works, addressing President Reagan's policies, were "lacking in any artistic merit"; Haacke knew how to interpret the verdict of this "bad" critic: "I take [it] as a compliment." "This condemnation puts me in the company of very good artists such Marcel Duchamp, Pollock and others who have earned his contempt. Kramer judged Duchamp's talents 'so weak that at times they come very close to being non-existent'. I also accept with pleasure his opinion that my works attack 'the idea of art itself'; his, of course" (p. 56). Because he quotes the critic's prose in very small pieces, Haacke does not allow us to see whether the critic had really compared him with Duchamp, but it has been learned that Bourdieu — who, when he performs his scientific sociology, affirms that his tastes in painting and music "correspond to [his] position in the social space"[5], is a great fan of Duchamp's gesture of displaying a urinal entitled "Fountain" in an exhibition, under cover of anonymity, using the museum "as a de-contextualizing context. That is, I take the urinal and, by virtue of placing it in a museum, I change its nature because the museum will operate on it the effect that museums exert on all the objects exhibited. . . It is a work of art to be contemplated" (p. 100).

What Bourdieu calls "outspokenness" is a mixture of philosophical arrogance and carelessness, or rather carelessness elevated by an intermittent philosophical hauteur. Whereas Bourdieu inflicts on us more and more Greek and Latin, in his writings, Hans Haacke, a subversive artist, uses (depending on the translation) words like guy, butt, pig, and bucks, probably to give us a sense of the "spontaneity" of their free exchange. He talks the same way about "Maggie's election campaigns" (p. 104), which is the stupidest kind of misogyny. Haacke says "Reagan", and "Bush", but when it comes to a woman Prime Minister, the diminutive is appropriate. He maintains that he supports the claims "of equality and respect for women and gays" (p. 63): the minimum respect would be to call them, in writing, by their names, as he does for men, not by a diminutive or the first name. Bourdieu, who "re-edited" this interview, did not see how crude the process was. What use to him was his great *pensum* on "male domination"?

In this *Free Exchange*, which sets itself the goal of being "outrageous", we come across trenchant assertions that would require a whole discussion on their own, vague assertions that cannot be proven, dubious "concepts", false comparisons, and base attacks; it is easy to give some examples. Haacke says, indignantly: "It was the first time since the beginning of the NEA in 1965[6] that political criteria were imposed on the deliberations of a jury of professionals, who until then had been the only ones to judge the institutions' and the artists' grant applications", and he enumerates, with the help of quotation marks, these political criteria: "representations of sadomasochism, homosexual eroticism, sexual exploitation of children. . ." (p. 14). Admittedly, this is dangerous ground, but can the fact that a law specifies that a public organization should not support works representing "the sexual exploitation of children" be called a "political criterion"? Haacke recalls that art is outside of "the prohibition on obscenity" as the Supreme Court affirmed (p. 16). But one must point out that a political authority has responsibilities that are different from those of an artist. And must the artist be subsidized, no matter what he does? The question is both serious and subtle.

There is no lack of vague but resolute assertions: Bourdieu is still shaking because a grant that he had once received (or was supposed to have received) from Kodak "caused an uproar" (p. 24). From whom, and in what form? What was extraordinary about it? Bourdieu represents himself unceasingly as repudiated, rejected, discredited, "a victim", forgetting — if we have to remind him — the Collège, the École des Hautes Études, his review, his published collections, his inclusion in the secondary school curriculum; a curious "victim" who exaggerates the aggressions. His accusations against his critics are as numerous as they are vague: he, a critical thinker ("critical" may be the only word he uses more frequently than "science") summarizes: "any critical thought [is] identified with Marxism and discredited" (p. 57). Haacke, who is not short on audacity, had just said: ". . . the label 'Marxist' plays almost the same role as the yellow star" (p. 56). This sentence is, and I choose the word carefully, ignoble. The artist (born in Germany, no less) should pay greater attention to what it means to say "wearing a yellow star", and he should think what happened to those who wore it, what it led to. And may we point out to the two thinkers — who do not risk anything, except making fools of themselves — that Marxist writings continue to make their way throughout the world and may we remind Bourdieu, definitely thoughtless, that just two years later he took on against "the vestiges of a Marxist vulgate which, beyond political affiliations, has clouded and confounded the brains of more than one generation".[7] Here is a proposition with which I fully agree.

When I said dubious concepts, I might have said concepts that are far from clear: for example, "the industry of the conscience". "From time to time I think", says Haacke, "that I have succeeded in producing works that serve as catalysts. . . Like it or not, every production of the industry of the conscience influences the social climate and, consequently, the political climate" (p. 30).

I mentioned false comparisons: "We are in a situation very similar to that of the painters of the Quattrocento, who had to fight to secure the freedom to choose, if not the subject, at least the 'manner'" (pp. 24-25). I find Bourdieu's sociology far removed from the current reality and cut off from the past. This comparison confirms that he is entirely cut off from history, that he has manufactured a history out of the pure interplay of ideas.

Finally, I mentioned base attacks. They are made indirectly. Just try to "follow" how Haacke, starting with the idea that there is a relationship between certain practices of republican governments and the Nazi ideology, goes on to name a "beneficiary" of money that smells of neo-conservatism and toxic gas: he has in mind the so greatly mourned historian, François Furet. Haacke says: "The cultural *Kampfblatt* of the neo-conservative movement is *The*

New Criterion" (p. 53). The German word was retained when the speech was translated into English; it means a written call to arms, more or less, but it is a veiled reference to something else: Haacke is implying that "the neo-conservatives"— Reagan, Bush — are not so far from. . . Nazism. For he had affirmed earlier that the president of the NEA, now responsible for how subsidies were granted, used a basic rule "that resembles the *gesundes Volksempfinden*, the term under which the Nazis purged the German museums of 'degenerate' art" (p. 15).

With considerable swagger, if I dare say so, he goes on to talk about the *New Criterion* and the fact that it receives support from four foundations "on the right", the "most faithful" of which is the Olin Foundation of New York. In passing, and without explaining why he mentions such "information", Haacke says that this "right-wing" foundation "which is one of the big American producers of ammunitions, including toxic gas", "subsidizes a significant number of institutes and professors in American universities, including at the University of Chicago": home of The John M. Olin Center for Inquiry into the Theory and Practice of Democracy, founded by Allan Bloom, and François Furet's John M. Olin Program in Political Culture (p. 54). The "cultural publications" of the French Communist Party were "thinking" and writing along these lines at the height of Stalinism.[8] In spite of that, Bourdieu vituperates against those who carry "political logic" over into literary and scientific life (p. 58), thus showing his inconsistency.

This free exchange oscillates between pontifical assertions and dubious generalities, sometimes both: these two thinkers are cocksure, they think they are infallible, and they are great B-S artists. Haacke, sharp of tongue and fuzzy of thought, says: "It is through this network [the four 'right-wing' foundations already cited, and other 'right-wing' foundations] that the neo-conservative movement articulates and provides political and strategic ideas to republican presidents. It is under the influence of Mr. Kristol that President Reagan adopted *supply side economics* — *Reaganomics* or *voodoo economics*, as George Bush called it when he was Reagan's rival and before he adopted it himself — which ruined the country" (p. 53). *Which ruined the country*, did he say? . . . Is Bourdieu, who spends his time telling us how to conduct ourselves, and telling us how to conduct science, satisfied with such a stupid thought? This recorded dialogue has been edited, gone over, "back and forth, over and over, which took a lot of time" (p. 9). How can we believe that Bourdieu's results are scientific, when he glosses over such gross absurdities? No doubt, overwhelmed by the cheeky glibness of the artist, the scientist forgot to reflect.

He does not go as far as the artist in making sweeping

generalities and pronouncing verdicts, but he complains plenty. "The concerted action of the conservative cliques (a detailed description, like your description of the group of intellectuals affiliated with the *New Criterion*, should be given of the *networks* of intellectuals, all associated with certain publications, who influence the intellectual life in France) gradually tends to impose an ideological climate, as you say, a doxa, a whole bunch of givens that are not discussed and that underlie every discussion; and which, once they are established, are terribly difficult to combat" (p. 58). The artist, the writer, the scientist have to intervene in "the battles of the century". "We are summoned all the more urgently to intervene in the world of men of power, business, and money, since they intervene more and more — and more and more effectively — in our world . . ." (p. 38).

But reading Bourdieu, one would think that artists, writers, and scientists must be extremely rare, for he bitterly criticizes the action of the "conservative cliques", the role of the brains behind big business and the affairs of State who invade philosophy and the social sciences, and the role of the intellectuals "who do as they do" (p. 39) — the intellectuals who "discuss all the problems of the day without a critical consciousness, technical skill or ethical conviction" (p. 59). To whom is he addressing himself, when he summons them to intervene in the battles of the century?

For, as we know, he has often said and he says more and more often, he feels alone, terribly alone; I cannot stop myself from quoting, again, the sentence in which he cursed the risks that he took: "I have often cursed the fate (or the logic) that forced to me to take up, with my eyes wide open, so weak a cause, to engage, with rational discourse as my only weapon, a battle that may have been lost before it began, against disproportionate social forces. . . ."[9] Has Bourdieu forgotten that David cut down Goliath with just one shot from his sling?

Attacking Jünger in connection with a prologue that he had written for the catalogue for the 45th International Art Exhibition in Venice, Bourdieu speaks ironically about his giving in to "compulsive repetition". In a complicated sentence, Bourdieu talks about "those who know how to read. . .", and he adds in a note, "They are probably very rare" (p. 118). Of course, he reads and knows how to read: if he says that Jünger was and is clearly an anti-Semite ("the old aesthete, having recovered from just about everything, except of course his soft spot for Nazism and anti-Semitism", p. 117) and if he says that his judgments are "priceless" (p. 119), we should believe him, since everything he says is scientific; he is Dr. Science. All the same, being anti-Semitic is so shameful and so frightful that Bourdieu should specify which of Jünger's writings or actions lead him to make that claim. Bourdieu talks and condemns without providing any references, any evidence to support the charges. He castigates certain magazines but does not name them; he attacks a novel by a former Maoist, but we do not know which one; he invokes the small fry of cultural activity, the 'poor whites' of culture, who have become an extremely virulent kind of cultural reactionaries (p. 69), about whom he says only that they "claim to be on the left". One might wish that he would be more specific. (Is he aiming, here, at the former Culture Minister, Jack Lang and his entourage?) He would retort that he (his science) does not condemn people but that he tries to render comprehensible to us the mechanisms and the operation of fields (artistic, literary, etc.), and that he wants to make us think about defending creative freedom, etc.. In fact, he is mostly attacking and denouncing, while claiming to be revealing and analyzing.

His criticism, which is generally aggressive, hardly appears to match the serenity of a scientific debate; furthermore, it is difficult to follow his "reasoning", his refutations, his accusations, his indignations, his impulses, which are by no means "sublimated" as he writes in *Pascalian Meditations*;[10] and it is hard to understand the appeals he launches into the vacuum, after all that he has just said about intellectuals who are lacking in "critical consciousness" and "technical skill", etc..

If he is so anxious to use only the weapons of rational discourse, why didn't Bourdieu teach Haacke how (he should) discuss, debate, and exchange? What are Baudrillard, A. D. Perrin, Furet, Lipman and his "buddy Podhoretz", Hilton Kramer, Montebello, Kristol, et al. supposed to do? The author of the preface announced that "This *Free Exchange*. . . is not afraid of naming names. . ." (p. 7.) Are they "the new multinational neo-conservative crusade" in Western culture? Then, what is this exchange? A scientific debate, with all the frankness that "should be the rule in intellectual exchanges",[11] thanks to Bourdieu the scientist, or a bunch of gossip, thanks to Hans Haacke, the artist? Bourdieu is priceless, I have begun to think, in the second sense: an extraordinary or very comic oddity.

Footnotes

1. Ines Champey, "Au lecteur (To the Reader)" in: Pierre Bourdieu, Hans Haacke, *Libre-échange,* Paris, Seuil/ Les Presses du réel, 1994, p. 5. The use of the word "scientist" is borrowed, of course, from P. Bourdieu, who abuses it.
2. P. Bourdieu and H. Haacke, *ibid.,* p. 9.
3. "Fieldwork in Philosophy", in *Choses dites,* Paris, Editions de Minuit, 1987, p. 13.
4. "Comment libérer les intellectuels libres (How can we free the free intellectuals?)", Interview with Didier Eribon, *Le Monde dimanche,* May 4, 1980, reprinted in *Questions de sociologie,* Paris, Editions de Minuit, 1980, p. 67.
5. Pierre Bourdieu, with Loïc J. D. Wacquant, *Réponses. Pour une anthropologie réflexive,* Paris, Le Seuil, 1992, p. 175.
6. The NEA (National Endowment for the Arts) is the federal administration for the support of the arts, in Washington.
7. Pierre Bourdieu, *Meditations pascaliennes,* Paris, Le Seuil, 1997, p. 16.
8. Hans Haacke proceeds by insinuation; for example, speaking of Arno Breker and a short interruption in his creative work, he adds: "Former comrades like [nine names are cited] needed busts" (p. 139). The word "comrade" is known to have very strong undertones in the language of the Nazis; where the word "friendly" would have sufficed (for example, Cocteau is cited here as a friend of Breker), he uses the word comrade, leaving us to think, "former Nazi".
9. *Méditations pascaliennes, op. cit.,* p. 15.
10. *Ibid,* p. 12.

    Without knowing who worked on, who wrote, page 4, this introduction of the book deserves attention. "Against the neo-conservative Multinationale of the new crusades of Western culture, destroyers of relativism and avant-gardism, against the perverse intrusions of State patronage, against the esthete nihilism of pseudo-revolutionaries, how can we affirm the independence of the critical intellectual and artist, who can bring to bear the most refined resources of formal research in the defense of creative freedom? How can we safeguard the outspokenness of this universe of free exchange which is (and which must) be the world of artists, writers and scientists? These are some of the questions discussed here by the artist and the sociologist, with the frankness that, according to them, ought to be the rule in all intellectual exchanges."

Chapter IX

“The Hope Of Efficacy”

On Television (1997)

We say far fewer original things than we think we do.
P. BOURDIEU, *On Television*, p. 23.

Speaking freely about television, on television, talking at length (in terms of time) and talking fast (in terms of substance), Bourdieu emphasized the very great dangers that television presents to the various spheres of cultural production — art, literature, science, philosophy and law, to political life and democracy, and he expressed the conviction that the analyses that he was making during a television broadcast would contribute “in some part, to changing things” (p. 63). Always very critical when he objectifies others — pundits or “fast-thinkers”, or journalists, “spokesmen for a typically petty bourgeois morality” (p. 52), etc., Bourdieu shows himself, by contrast, “irredeemably” (as Lenin would say) optimistic in assessing the value of his “intervention”. “By raising the awareness of the mechanisms, [the sociologist] can help give a little freedom to people who are manipulated by these mechanisms, be they journalists or television viewers. I think (in parentheses) that if journalists who may feel objectified, as they say, if they listen carefully to what I say, they will come to acknowledge — at least, I hope so — that, by clarifying things that they understand vaguely but that they do not want to understand too well, I give them instruments of freedom to govern the mechanisms to which I am referring" (p. 63). Although he says, repetitively, that he never feels really "justified" in existing as an intellectual, in every one of his "analyses" and his "interventions" Bourdieu tells us how useful and effective his work is, how his discourse is autonomous, free, critical, conclusive. . . He exposes the true meaning of his action: he is "giving weapons" to the dominated, etc., he is "giving them freedom", etc.. Note that scientists do not tell the readers what they owe them, in every article they produce. . . This insistence on the efficacy of sociological science should be a tip off to the reader.

After *On Television* was published, Bourdieu must have felt misunderstood once again, misread — for example, when he learned that Régis Debray (after saluting what he called Bourdieu's "justified" prestige) wrote that if this had been a student's paper, it would have received a poor grade. He said he smiled at all the clichés, unattributed borrowings, invectives transformed into verdicts, personal obsessions presented as objective statements, and the tone of a Papal encyclical used as the vehicle for fulmination and excommunication.[1] Régis Debray was probably swatting this fly because it really did "bug" him, and also, perhaps, because the encyclical tone, common with Bourdieu, became even more incongruous given the subject and the scant analysis. Passing yourself off as Science personified when you have the institution behind you, said Debray, is an old war, it is "the immemorial war of clerics in the city" but, he added, it shows disrespect for democratic values. It seems to me that people extremely rarely take such advantage of their positions of authority in the university milieu, and it seems me that the war of the clerics throughout the course of history has generally mobilized only second-rate clerics, those who wanted to move up, to gain recognition. But in this case, where would he move up? Bourdieu has every form of recognition. . . Moreover, there is no war in this case, only the soliloquy of a demiurge.

The critics' indignation against the booklet surprised me, initially; the text seemed to me to be of little interest, often trivial. Re-reading it, one sees that many of the quirks that were present in the preceding works are laid out here for all to see. How can I summarize this lesson that Bourdieu says was conceived as an *intervention* (his emphasis)? The desire "to be understood by everyone" obliged him, he says, "on more than one occasion, to simplify, or make approximations" (p. 6). "Approximations" we may readily concede to him, but they are not due to the simplicity of his language: on the contrary, he has amply shown how complexity, "artifice", and technicality of language permit considerable approximation. . . He chatters authoritatively and disorganizedly about intellectuals who agree to speak on television — even without giving any thought to the conditions of their participation (!); about economic and political censorship and self-censorship, about the pernicious "symbolic violence" (p. 16) that television exerts, about the "ratings mentality", about the journalistic field, about the talking heads, people of the agora — always in a hurry — the contrary of the philosopher, who has time. Bourdieu, once more, calls upon his dear Plato: "He says, more or less, that, when you are in a hurry, you cannot think" (p. 30), a point of view that appeared "aristocratic" to him, even while he was affirming that the link between thought and time was indisputable.

No doubt Bourdieu is right in saying, "Television is not very favorable to the expression of thought", for, speaking on television, he winds up saying: "Television has a kind of monopoly, in fact, on the formation of the minds of a great majority of the population" (p. 17), and then twenty pages further on he says that in the 1960's, "a certain number of 'sociologists' (with a plethora of quotation marks) rushed to say that television, as a 'means of mass communication' would lead to standardization. Television was supposed to level, to homogenize all the TV viewers, little by little. In fact, they underestimated the capacities of resistance" (pp. 39-40). Thus, television forms the minds but the minds resist. Is this what Bourdieu has discovered?

How does his analysis clarify things, how can it change them? He goes on at length, for example, about the concerns one should have, the precautions one should take, before agreeing to speak on television. For him, obviously, "the intellectuals", "some of our philosophers", do not ask themselves the right questions, the necessary questions; many of them participate "only to show off and to be seen". "Today, the television screen has become a kind of Narcissus's mirror, a narcissistic exhibition space" (p. 11). If Bourdieu took a moment to think, he would notice that most intellectuals, those who produce writings, who devote all their time, all their strength and all their passion to that, speak on television very seldom and that the few writers who do appear there frequently are not very representative of the intellectual world. And since he says that participating in a TV show is a very important issue, he ought to analyze for us his appearance on television with Abbot Pierre [founder of a French charity, along the lines of the Salvation

Army]. He should consider whether he was really there to say something and whether he really said it, whether he really "gave back to everyone" what was achieved through his research, which is the scientist's "mission", and "particularly urgent" for the sciences of society (p. 12).

After this warning to intellectuals, his remarks on censorship (economic and otherwise) are quite banal and he admits it, but he says he is going to reveal a secret later on (?), he will reveal the "anonymous, invisible mechanisms, through which censorship of all kinds is exerted, making television a formidable instrument for maintaining symbolic law and order" (p. 14). Having announced his effort in *enunciating* the mechanisms, he underlines, informs, insists, etc.: his effort is not an effort of *denunciation* (p. 15). This exemplifies two characteristics of Bourdieu's prose: playing with words and sounds, and giving great weigh to announcing the work that he is going to produce, how wonderful and efficacious it is, rather than to the analysis and the results.

Of course, he attacks Jacques Julliard, Claude Imbert, Jacques Attali, Serge July, Jean-Marie Cavada, André Comte-Sponville and many others by name, but he has already emphasized that journalists should not feel they are being "nailed" (p. 15): he is merely offering an analysis, not a criticism addressed to people; he would never look to rail against one or another specific person. . . However, they are going to feel that they are being criticized because — you guessed it — that is a way of "defending oneself against analysis", in short, this is an instance of the famous resistance.[2]

Bourdieu can thus make whatever statements he wishes; he can be dogmatic and banal about everything. For example, the effect of reality (he underlines it, he puts it in italics, he defines it) is that the image "can make you perceive and make you believe what it makes you perceive", it can serve to get people in action, and he explains at great length: "Various facts, everyday incidents or accidents, can be charged with political, ethical, etc. implications that are likely to spark strong, often negative feelings like racism, xenophobia, the fear-hatred of foreigners, and the simple fact of *recording*, of *reporting* on something always implies a social construction of reality that can exert social effects of mobilization (or of demobilization)" (p. 21). All that is very well known, and has often been analyzed. Although Bourdieu "reveals" the journalists' game of mirrors, mutually reflecting themselves and going on at length about other newspapers, which produces "a formidable wall-like effect, a mental restriction" (p. 25), through his lessons on television, he himself gives an example of the "wall effect": he quotes himself, he quotes three of his "followers" and he ignores everything that has been written on this subject — or at least, he doesn't mention a word about it.

His analysis of the "TV ratings mentality" covers well-worn terrain; by the same token, his criticism of debates is banal, as is what he has to say about how the show is composed. "It is determinant. It is an invisible work and the show itself is the result of it. For example, take all the background work involved in the invitation process: there are people whom one does not think of inviting; and people whom one invites and who refuse. The show is what you see, and what you see hides what you do not see: one does not see, in a constructed perception, the social conditions of the construction" (p. 37). Does he really think he is telling us something we don't know, here?[3]

He contrasts the bad hosts (who allocate the time slots, who set the "tone" of the shows, etc.) to the good way that he and his team, as represented in *The Weight of the World*, approach interviews: the "know-how" that they demonstrate, their demonstration that they "know how" to conduct interviews: to whom is he speaking? Still to the dim-witted people that he takes us to be; he explains that he and his team know that the people they are questioning expect certain signs of interest, a "yes, yes", a nod of the head, etc. during the interview (p. 35), and so on. He declares and emphasizes how extremely "important, from the point of view of democracy" are debates, where "the speakers are not all equal", and even "extraordinarily unequal" (!) (p. 36). To restore just "a very little bit of equality", he explains that the talk show host should be "unequal", i.e. should do what he himself did during the surveys for *The Weight of the World*, that "work that helped draw out people's words". "The thing is to lend yourself to the service of somebody whose words are important, where we want to know what he has to say and how he thinks, and help him articulate it. However, that is not at all what the hosts do" (p. 37).

The entire lesson on the show (and on the non-show — what happens behind the scenes) is a stream of banalities; the "hidden truths" that are revealed are well-known, and he overlooks or ignores much else. He takes on the *fast-thinkers*, "thinkers who think faster than their shadows. . ." (p. 30), specialists in "throw-away thoughts" (p. 38), who "offer *cultural junk-food*" (p. 31), who talk "all the time" (p. 36), and he finds it necessary to reel in Plato and Descartes. Plato allows him to point out the negative link between haste and thought (p. 30), and Descartes serves to demonstrate what would be "the *thinking* thought", which is "by definition, subversive" (?), and the "deployment" of which is "intrinsically linked to the times"; "We must unfurl a series of propositions connected by 'thus', 'consequently', 'all that being said', . . ." (p. 31). And it is Plato again who helps him to conclude: Plato said that "we are puppets of the divine. In the universe of television, one has the impression that the social agents, despite their appearing to be important, free, and autonomous . . . are puppets of a need that should be described, of a structure that we must release and bring forth" (p. 42). The second lesson proposes to bring forth the invisible structure and its effects.

Bourdieu then utilizes a concept that he considers to be "a little bit technical", the concept of the field, and he "brutally" — for once, he admits it and says so (p. 48) — describes the ongoing battles to preserve or transform that field of forces that is the media field, while recalling, between parentheses, that to be complete, we *ought to* take into account the position of this national field in the global field (!): and he *should*, he'll *have to*, tell us how to do it. . .

In his two lessons, Bourdieu takes his time telling us simple things, and he speaks with great haste about extremely difficult things. For "these are very complicated things where one can really advance knowledge only through very great empirical work" (p. 58). Not having visibly invested the empirical work about which he talks at every opportunity, he deplores that historians do not do enough such work, on journalism in particular (would he use such work? how?), he makes fun of "a non-existent science": media-ology (p. 58), and he "brutally" evokes the battle arbitrated by the TV ratings — fearsome, demagogic and antidemocratic as they are, and the influence of television. Criticizing the fact that one might be satisfied with mere polemics, with attacking the leaders (like, by the way, the ubiquitous Karl Kraus whom he so admires[4]), he reminds us that we must understood that in the universe of journalism, the men and the women who are responsible "are largely defined in their possibilities and their impossibilities by the structure in which they are placed and by the position that they occupy within this structure" (p. 62). In other words, Bourdieu takes the subject he is treating and automatically dresses it in his theory, a kind of wild card that is good in everything situation.

At moments, he turns pessimistic; for example, he harps on the intrusion of media power, that is, the power that is "economically tied to the media, by the media, in the universe of the purest science" (p. 70). "When it comes to apparently independent disciplines, like history or anthropology, or biology and physics, the influence of the media becomes increasingly significant insofar as obtaining grants may depend, we no longer know how much, on celebrity that is dependent on media recognition and one's reputation among one's peers" (p. 70). He says that he could offer many examples, but he gives only one; has he analyzed cases where obtaining grants in physics or anthropology, for example, could and did depend on media celebrity?

At other times, he is optimistic. His analyses can contribute to changing things, he said at the beginning of the game; they "may give tools or weapons to everyone who, in the professions related to the image itself, are fighting to keep what could have been an extraordinary instrument of direct democracy from being converted into an instrument of symbolic oppression" (p. 8).

At the beginning of the first lesson, Bourdieu says that he wants to reach an audience that would be broader than the ordinary public, and he explains in the second lesson that it is necessary "to defend both the esotericism that is inherent (by definition) to any search into the avant-garde and the need to exotericize the esoteric"[5] (pp. 76-77). He ardently dreams of sociology becoming an autonomous field, like mathematics, but alas! woe is me, everyone keeps butting in. "Mr. Peyrefitte intends to give me lessons in sociology" (p. 71). "To gain autonomy, we must build that kind of ivory tower inside of which one judges oneself, one criticizes oneself, one even fights oneself, but with full knowledge of the facts" (id.), therefore it is necessary to defend "maintaining and even making greater the barriers to entry into the fields of production" (p. 76). He insists that sociology has problems owing to the fact that "the barriers to entry are too low"; he thus suggests increasing them, and he also suggests "increasing the *barrier to exit*" (p. 76). [Not giving in to haste, I started to think about this "exit barrier": isn't this what has led critics to keep a low profile, to keep quiet, even respectful, vis-à-vis Bourdieu, armed with a reinforced exit barrier?(!), even if he says that he wishes that this duty would be accompanied by "an amelioration" of the conditions of exit . . .]

We must, says Bourdieu, defend "the conditions of production that are necessary to make the universal progress, and at the same time, we must work to generalize the conditions of access to the universal, to make it so that more and more people meet the conditions necessary to appropriate the universal". Repeating, and underscoring, one of his pet peeves — the restitution of a "complex" idea is difficult — he invites the producers to come out of their citadels and to fight alongside the teachers, the trade unions, and the associations [a vague, broad term] "so that the receivers receive an education that aims at raising their level of reception" (p. 77). For one must never forget the principle meaning of Bourdieu's works and public actions: "I defend the conditions necessary to the production and the diffusion of the highest creations of humanity" (p. 76). Nothing less than that.

This is surely one of most disturbing aspects of Bourdieu's discourse; it is disturbing because it rings false: locked up in his little citadel where, in his eyes, the only residents are those who think (with his thought), and who do not manifest any resistance to his scientific results, he only comes out to impose his "thoughtful thought", refusing to engage in discussion. His citadel has nothing to do with the ideal scholarly city wished for in *The Craft of Sociology*, a city where one might dream of increasing criticism and the exchange of information, breaking down the epistemological isolation maintained by the compartmentalization of institutions and reducing the obstacles to communication related to the hierarchy of renown and status, to the diversity of education and careers. . ."[6] Bourdieu's morals and ambitions cannot make us believe that he wants to work for "the universalization of the conditions of access to the universal" (p. 77).

Speaking, once more, of the sociologist as somebody who is "disturbing", he tells us why: "It is because he obliges us to make conscious things that one prefers to leave unconscious" (p. 60). What has he made conscious here?

Footnotes

1. Régis Debray, "Savants contre docteurs (Scientists against doctors)", *Le Monde,* March 18, 1997. All the words that I reprise here to summarize Debray's article are words that he uses.
2. *Addition:* Pierre Bourdieu has just published two more texts to round out this opuscule. In a postface published in the English edition of *On Television,* he speculates about the meaning "of the extreme violence of the reactions" incited by his analysis. "The 'Big Guns' who have taken exception to my book purely and simply disregarded the method that is at work in it (and in particular my analysis of the journalistic world as a field), thus reducing it, without even knowing they were so doing, to a series of banal viewpoints and positions, interlaced with bursts of polemics." "La télévision, le journalisme et la politique", reprinted in *Contre-feux,* Paris, Liber-Raisons d'agir, 1998, p. 76 and p. 77.
   In the French version of an interview published in Rio de Janeiro, in connection with this opuscule which had just come out in Brazil, Bourdieu said he finds evidence of journalists' "double conscience" in the reactions of "the Big Guns" who "have unanimously and violently condemned" his book, "trying to outdo each other in saying that it did not offer anything that was not already known". He affirmed that sociologists (like him) can provide journalists with "instruments of knowledge and comprehension, and possibly of action, that would enable them to work effectively to control the economic and social forces that control them. . . " "Retour sur la télévision", in *Contre-feux, op. cit.,* p. 85 and p. 88.
3. Bourdieu's generalities on "the perceived" built on the show is a laughing matter. I'm no specialist on television, but in 1985 I was involved in the preparations for a broadcast on Channel 2 about film on the Manouchian scandal (I had been consulted by one of Armand Jammot's collaborators), and I gave my reactions in *Libération*: "The Manouchian Affair, the Show as a Screen" (June 29-30, 1985). Clearly, what this title summarizes is how a show is composed; and I described how the show was crafted, this time by the Communist Party, which retained "the right to judge, to inform, and to display the truth of the day". The conditions under which television

shows are put together are well known and they have been described often.

4. Isn't the evocation of Karl Kraus quite simply hypocrisy? "One cannot, one must not be satisfied with denouncing the leaders. For example, Karl Kraus, the great Viennese satirist, took on very violently the equivalent of what today would be the director of *le Nouvel Observateur*: he spent his time denouncing his cultural conformity that was so destructive to culture, his tolerance for minor or miserable writers, and the discredit that he threw on pacifist ideas by professing them hypocritically. . ." (p. 62).
5. The word "avant-garde" needs to be defined; Bourdieu's frequent use of this term, as well as of the words "subversion" and "transgression", casts doubt on the scientificity of his language.
6. "Cité savante et vigilance épistémologique (The Learned City and Epistemological Vigilance)", in: Pierre Bourdieu, Jean-Claude Chamboredon, Jean-Claude Passeron, *Le Métier de sociologue,* Paris, Mouton/Bordas,1968, pp. 111-112.

CONCLUSION
ON THE FUTURE OF SCIENCE

I was just wondering which topic to make the focus of this conclusion — Bourdieu and Marxism, Bourdieu and science, Bourdieu and intellectuals? — when *Libération* published three pages on "Bourdieu's little books", Bourdieu's networks, and the "thunderous" launching of his publishing house[1]. . . Reading the article, I concluded that I had been very naive in taking Bourdieu seriously; I had devoted months to reading him and re-reading him, full-time(!); and I had striven to show, and to document, that despite all his proclamations of being scientific, his sociology was nothing but an ideological discourse.

I could very well have concluded my critical reading by applying to Bourdieu his own criticism of Montesquieu's theory of climates and of "the logic of the mode of argumentation" employed to make something look like a truth: the [Bourdieusian] theory is "a remarkable paradigm of '*scientific*' *mythology*, a discourse founded in belief (or prejudice) that is inclined toward science and that is characterized by the co-existence of *two intermingled principles of coherence*: a scientifically appealing proclaimed coherence, which affirms itself by displaying a plethora of external signs of being scientific, and a hidden coherence that is fundamentally mythical. This kind of talk, playing a double game and intending to be understood on two levels, owes both its social existence and its effectiveness to the fact that, in the age of science, the unconscious impulse that inclines us to give socially important problems a monolithic and total answer, like myths or religions, can be satisfied only by borrowing the modes of thought or expression of science".[2] This analysis was fairly serious, I thought... However, now I am wondering, why did I take so much trouble when "the scientist" himself was taking it easy?

Bourdieu's editor, the head of Le Seuil publishing house, said to a journalist from *Libération:* "He felt something in the public, in particular among the young people: a need to speak out, to mirror their irritation and their rebellion..." One of the pillars of his networks, Patrick Champagne, was to the point: "Look at the success of *Charlie Hebdo* these days... We are in the same state of mind: [we want] to be there, to say what we think, to refuse the consensus, to play at being bloody nuisances." And Christophe Charle made reference to the little Maspero collection in the 1960's and 1970's.[3] Today, Pierre Bourdieu wants to be "a militant scientist". As Patrick Champagne recalled so vigorously: "To art, sociology is not art." Let us grant that his publications have amply made that point, and so have Bourdieu's.

From "his modern and well-lit office at the College of France", Bourdieu thus lobs his "little books of protest" — "clear, short, accessible, punchy, affordable", as the journalist reports; he wages a major battle and a general resistance (against the neoliberal plague, conservative revolutions, restorations, the destruction of a civilization, the myth of globalization — and also against Philippe Sollers[4]), he militates, furbishes and provides useful "weapons", "rehabilitates the polemic" (whereas he had always cherished and practiced it), in short, he is preparing, on the European scale, "a left of the Left".[5]

The journalist from *Libération* adds to the description of the Bourdieu networks functioning "full steam", a report on Bourdieu's last little book, *Acts of Resistance: Against the Tyranny of the Market. Resistance* and *fight* have become central words in Bourdieu's thought, supplanting the words *science* and *critical.* But the two epochs have something in common: the scientist and the scientific militant both provide "useful weapons". It is because he wants to "serve" and thinks he does serve that Bourdieu "is resolved" to publish every word he says; he feels "constrained to do so, by a kind of legitimate fury, sometimes akin to something like a feeling of indebtness".[6] He thinks he is "creating the conditions for a collective work of rebuilding of a universe of realistic ideals, that can mobilize the will without mystifying the consciousness".[7]

It is quite imprudent in a conclusion to tackle Bourdieu's latest writing — given that he is now publishing everything that he says, there is a considerable risk that in the next three or four weeks I will come across yet another slender volume of his words of wisdom. . . nonetheless, I will take my chances and talk about it, because this collection acknowledges and reflects the impotence of Bourdieusian sociology.

This sociology was characterized by a furious will for deconstruction [in fact, for destruction]: school, art, and philosophy were, he said, revealed for what they are; that is, they were tried, caricatured — and condemned. Bourdieusian theory, child of a watered-down Marxism with a strong dose of Leninism, repeats itself with great confidence, copies itself over and over, parodies itself; he must have begun to feel, some time ago, that it was inadequate. That Bourdieu invented "the 'torn' *habitus*" in *The*

Weight of the World. Dare I mention that if his central concept of "the *habitus*" seems to have turned out to be flawed, it would appear to indicate that he may be starting to wake up or, at least, to feel a certain discomfort.[8] Now, Bourdieu wants to develop forms of resistance, to forge alliances; he appeals to the European trade unions and the associations, he wants to invent new forms of communication, he wants to instigate an international mobilization of intellectuals, etc.; he asks researchers to change their language and their state of mind, he wants to give everyone "reasons to act"... After his phase of raging deconstruction, he is frantically seeking to rebuild. In contrast to "the tight budgets and shortsightedness" of the bankers, the tax inspectors, the nobility of the State, etc., he proposes "an economy of happiness"[9], a new word for Bourdieu, now that the fantasies that had nourished his theory have turned out to be glaucous and desperate.

In recent years, Bourdieu has turned again to philosophy and has renewed an ambiguous flirtation with it. He, who at one time lectured the engaged intellectual, now fumes over the "integrated" intellectuals, the "disengaged" intellectuals. Whatever the purported subject, whatever the audience and venue of his speech, Bourdieu takes the intellectuals to task and lectures them on what they should do. Touching vaguely on "the myth of globalization", before an audience of Greek workers, he ends his speech by challenging the intellectuals, saying that even though they are dominated by the dominant, the intellectuals are part of the dominant — and he states that that is one of the reasons for their ambivalence, for their lukewarm engagement in the battle.[10]

Lukewarm engagement? If we take a look at the writers of innovative, powerful works, committed to the long term (Fernand Braudel, Claude Lévi-Strauss, Paul Bénichou, Jean Bottéro, Louis Dumont and Georges Devereux, for example, and dozens of others), we note that they did not "engage". Engagement, without exception, takes the place of "work" among those producers whose work is feeble or of little interest, or has yet to come to fruition. And since he invented the "negative intellectual"[11], Bourdieu should take a look at the signatories of the "intellectuals' appeal in support of the strikers" (December 1995), of which he was the heart and soul, and perhaps the author. Are they positive intellectuals?[12]

A Brazilian journalist, referring to Umberto Eco's dichotomy, asked Bourdieu: "Can one say that you are an 'apocalyptic', against the 'integrated'? Bourdieu responded: "You could say that. Many are 'integrated', indeed." According to him, the "integrated", throughout the world, are increasingly selling out to or are seduced by the established order[13]. One of Bourdieu's innumerable contradictions is that he relentlessly summons the intellectuals and assigns them formidable tasks of protest and resistance, and yet he sees them as "integrated"; even their possible revolt is not glorious but corporatist, petty. "When they revolt, it is still (as it was in Germany in 1933) because they think they are not getting their due, given their competence, guaranteed by their diplomas."[14] Reading that, one wonders why Bourdieu is so courageous, or even so stoical, to continue living immersed in such a lamentable environment.

By adopting the position of the engaged intellectual (of course, not a "lukewarm" engagement), Bourdieu made his sociology very clear. It is, as he has always said, a science that is not much liked, it is a poorly understood, disturbing science. But he did everything possible to lead the gropings (often food for thought) of the incipient sociology toward a militant discourse that was not even new or "modern". His sociology repeated that it meant to be useful and effective (and he thought that it was); it meant to be useful, to arm the people. . . What scientist asks himself every morning whether his research is useful, whether it will find an immediate application? The ways by which knowledge is transmitted are difficult to know, to analyze and especially to envisage and plan.

Having broken society into two camps — the dominant and the dominated — and having defined the intellectual as a dominant-dominated, Bourdieu has been talking out of both sides of his mouth.

One of the ongoing tricks that his sociology plays is that it says two different things at the same time: that the Director of Studies at the EHESS (the School for Advanced Studies, in Paris) and a professor at the College of France are dominant-dominateds is indisputable, it is scientific. He has told us many times, for example, that he never talks about his "tastes" in painting or in music because his "tastes" "correspond to [his] position in the social space."[15] But when he wants to impose his opinions and fantasies as scientific facts, sociologist Bourdieu goes back to his *habitus* of origin (i.e. that which was derived from his original class situation, and experienced within a certain type of family structure. . . that of a dominated-excluded young person from the Béarn. His original *habitus* "forgets" (or overcomes) all the restructurings of later experiences when he talks, for example, about the tastes of the popular classes or the misery of the world, or the railwaymen's strike.

Intellectuals are products of the elite universities and graduate programs, etc., and these institutions transform and restructure the primary *habitus*, inculcating new dispositions, etc. (as he has explained endlessly). Apparently, Bourdieu has started to recall (in manner that appears rather excessive) his "origins" (which, by the way, is quite vague — what is the source of his complaints: the fact of having been born in a remote "province"? or the socio-professional family milieu?), only so that he can present his fantasies as social "justifications" and demolish every critic; his adversaries are inevitably examples of the "integrated", even if they call themselves "critics" or quite simply Leftists; the truth is that they have all sided with the established order.[16]

The reasoning behind both Bourdieu's "theory" and his rhetoric of intimidation, his ardor in managing his business and his political choices (which are really not very well-considered[17]) is in fact, in the long run, untenable. His vociferous political engagement today, following on the heels of a form of engagement that claimed to be radically scientific, shows us the fundamental meaning of his sociological work. It is a rancorous vision of the social world, a fearful struggle masking itself as audacity.

His theory, a sophisticated and very partial reprise of Marxism-Leninism, had already done a poor job of accounting for the society of the 1960's-1970's. The rapid and sweeping transformations of the 1980's made it still more inadequate. Militancy, which is never realistic, enables him to believe that he has some control over the present. Attacking (after a prudent delay) the negative role of the

Marxist vulgate (and Althusser), which "clouded and confounded the brains of more than one generation"[18], he himself takes up the role of clouding and confounding, with assurance and a perfectly clear conscience.

Bourdieu recently affirmed that he resists occasions when he might be drawn into going beyond the limits of his competence, due to the situation or a sense of solidarity.[19] Really, he never put up enough resistance. His conference in East Berlin, fifteen days before the Berlin Wall came down (an analysis that he published in 1994[20]), his judgment on the collapse of the Soviet-style regimes (a collapse which he declares to have been "unhoped-for", thus demonstrating the limits of his understanding of history[21], and his comparisons (that go against all reason) with the rise of Nazism, destroy the credibility of his reminders and his reflections on the need for the "critical intellectual" and "the immense historical responsibility" of the intellectuals — although he also judges that they are not all, and are not always, up to these responsibilities.[22] What does he mean by "critical intellectuals" — he cites Marx, Nietzsche, Sartre, Foucault — and how does he define their historical responsibility?

Ten years after the collapse of the Soviet bloc, younger generations, unaware of this so horrible very recent past and often disoriented by the new reality — unemployment, the rifts and the latent confrontations of our society — are eager to believe a prophet whose impassioned, furious remarks, dressed in all the trappings of science, are guaranteed by the title of Professor at the College of France. I do not believe that intellectuals are a countervailing power "of the first order", that they have an "immense" responsibility; but of course, they do have one responsibility. Pierre Bourdieu, in all his demolishing, attacking, denouncing, and in all his supporting, flattering, and alternating bouts of demagoguery and threats, fails to fulfill that which he says is the function of the "creative" professionals: "public utility and sometimes public salvation".[23]

Footnotes

1. Antoine de Gaudemar, "Les petits pavés de Bourdieu (Bourdieu's Little Books)", *Libération,* April 16, 1998.
2. Pierre Bourdieu, "Le Nord et le Midi : contribution à une analyse de l'effet Montesquieu (The North and South of France: A contribution to an analysis of the Montesquieu effect)", *Actes de la recherche en sciences sociales,* No. 35, November 1980; reprinted in *Ce que parler veut dire,* Paris, Fayard, 1982, under the title: "La rhétorique de la scientificité : contribution à une analyse de l'effet Montesquieu", pp. 227-239. Citation, p. 228.
3. For the benefit of younger readers, let's recall that the authors of Maspero's "Little Collection" were mostly Mao Zedong, Ho Chi Minh, Che Guevara, Frantz Pennon, Malcolm X, Fidel Castro, Charles Bettelheim, Pierre Jalée, Louis Althusser, Etienne Balibar, G. Lukacs, et al..
   So here we have *Liber-Raisons d'agir* taking its place between *Charlie-Hebdo* and Maspero's thinkers. Bourdieu has been quoting one of Karl Kraus's sayings for some time now, and very often: "when choosing between two evils, I refuse to accept the lesser one". Nonetheless, history as we know it leads me to recommend to Bourdieu that he prefer (nevertheless) *Charlie-Hebdo* over Mao Zedong.
4. Pierre Bourdieu, "Sollers tel quel (Sollers just as he is)", *Libération,* January 27, 1995, reprinted in *Contre-feux,* Paris, Liber-Raisons d'agir, 1998, pp. 18-20. This polemical article holds the reader's attention only because Bourdieu announced that all the texts that he has brought together in this book provide "useful weapons to all those who endeavor to resist the neoliberal plague". Really? Does he think that Philippe Sollers is the equivalent of . . . Hans Tietmeyer, head of the Bank of Germany? On this last, see: "La pensée Tietmeyer (Tietmeyer's thinking)", *Contre-feux, op. cit.,* pp. 51-65 (Lecture at the University of Freiburg, October 1996).
5. Cf. also: Pierre Bourdieu, "Pour une gauche de gauche", *Le Monde,* April 8, 1998 (p. 1). A footnote says that this text was written by four researchers and academics: all that work to come up with an article that talks about the "fascist-ization of part of the political class and of French society", of "a

creeping or declared fascist-ization", of "the murky origins" of the Fifth Republic, "the neoliberal troika Blair-Jospin-Schroeder", comparing the French right with the German right and center in the early 1930s, "with its extremist inclinations", and concluding with a call for international resistance to neoliberalism.

Bourdieu speaks of "the sad spectacle of our political-media news-casters; what a sad spectacle to see a professor of the College of France using his "consecration" to sign a militant leaflet, ignoring history, fascism, Germany of the 1930s.

6. Bourdieu, "To The Reader", *Contre-feux, op. cit.,* p. 7.
7. "La main gauche et la main droite de l'Etat (The left hand and the right hand of the State)", interview, *Le Monde,* January 4, 1992, reprinted in *Contre-feux, op. cit.,* p. 17.
8. How better to denote this derision than by evoking dear Meilhac and Halévy: "his pants had split" — for, in his hundreds of pages of definitions and redefinitions of the *habitus*, Bourdieu wrote: "It is their present and past position in the social structure that the individuals — understood as physical people — carry with them, at all times and in all places, *in the form of the habitus which they wear like clothes* and which, like clothes, make the man, i.e. the social person. . . ." *Esquisse d'une théorie de la pratique,* Paris/Genève, Droz, 1972, p. 184 [italicized by J.V. - L.].
9. "Le mythe de la 'mondialisation' et l'Etat social européen", *Contre-feux, op. cit.,* p. 46. (Lecture to the General Confederation of Greek Workers, Athens, October 1996.)
10. *Ibid,* p. 50.
11. "L'intellectuel négatif", *Contre-feux, op. cit.,* pp. 105-107. This article is written against one specific writer, but fails to give the name. Bourdieu says that this text, written in January 1998, "was not published" [until April 1998].
12. One of the little books from the Liber-Raisons d'agir publishing house is on *The "December" of French Intellectuals* (1998, J. Duval, C. Gaubert, F. Lebaron, D. Marchetti, F. Pavis). It's worth reading, although it can be boring since the unknowns are so legion among the signatories of the petition "in support of the strikers", but which describes the preparation of this action (or intervention) and the role of Pierre Bourdieu.
13. "Retour sur la télévision", interview published in *O Globo,*

Rio de Janeiro, October 4, 1997, reprinted in *Contre-feux, op. cit.,* p. 90.

14. "Le mythe de la 'mondialisation'. . ." *article cit,* p. 50.
15. Pierre Bourdieu, with Loïc J. D. Wacquant, *Réponses. Pour une anthropologie réflexive,* Paris, Le Seuil, 1992, p. 175.
16. "Retour sur la télévision", *interview cit.,* p. 90.
17. Having formed the habit of talking about everything, Bourdieu has no time to reflect: remember that he says, recalling, of course, Plato, "in haste, one cannot think".
    Examples of his unwise remarks: ". . . without for an instant thinking of making a link between the Front National and the IMF" (La pensée Tietmeyer", *article cit.,* p. 57.)
    "I give all this food for thought to those who, quiet or indifferent today, will come, in thirty years' time, to express their 'repentance', when the young French of Algerian origin will have the first name Kelkal" ("These 'leaders' who call us irresponsible", *Inrockuptibles,* 8 October 1997, reprinted in *Contre-feux, op. cit.,* pp. 93-94).
    "The negative intellectual has fulfilled his mission: who will wish to be in solidarity with murderers, rapists and assassins — especially when we designate such people, without any historical basis, as 'madmen of Islam', cloaked under the pejorative name of 'Islamist', a condensation of all Eastern fanaticisms, carefully crafted to give racist distrust the indisputable alibi of ethical and secular legitimacy?" ("L'intellectuel négatif", *article cit.,* p. 106.)
18. Pierre Bourdieu, *Méditations pascaliennes,* Paris, Le Seuil, 1997, p. 16.
19. Pierre Bourdieu, *Contre-feux, op. cit.,* p. 7.
20. Pierre Bourdieu, "La variante 'soviétique' et le capital politique (The 'Soviet' alternative and political capital)", conference given in East Berlin on October 25, 1989, *Raisons pratiques,* Paris, Le Seuil, 1994, pp. 31-35 (see our Chapter 5, note 12).
21. Here, Bourdieu exposes the limits of his political sense and also shows evidence of a very restricted vision: As a director at the EHESS for more than thirty years, hadn't he been familiar with Fernand Braudel? Didn't he have occasions to discuss with him, and especially to listen? I met Fernand Braudel several times in 1982, to question him on the intellectual climate of the 1950s, in connection with my thesis on the

Communist Party and the culture of 1944 - 1956. He talked about Communism in general and in April 1982, he said to me firmly that the USSR was going to break down, before the end of the century without any doubt and he added, almost dreamily: it is so contrary to nature. From that day onward, I looked differently at everything that was being written about the USSR. I cannot believe that Fernand Braudel gave his verdict as a historian to me alone.

22. "La main gauche et la main droite de l'Etat", *interview cit.,* p. 16.
23. *Ibid,* p. 17.

Selected Works by Pierre Bourdieu

Titles are listed in English, if available, followed by the original French title.

Actes de la recherche en sciences sociales.

Acts of Resistance: Against the Tyranny of the Market / translated by Richard Nice. New York: New Press: Distributed by Norton, c1998.
Contre-feux. Editions Liber-Raisons d'Agir. Paris.

Academic Discourse. Linguistic Misunderstanding and Professorial Power Pierre Bourdieu, Jean-Claude Passeron, and Monique De Saint Martin; With Contributions By Christian and Guy Vincent; translated by Richard Teese. 136 p. Calif: Stanford University Press, 1994
Rapport Pédagogique et communication 127 p. Paris, La Haye, Mouton et Cie., 1968

The Algerians. Translated by Alan C. M. Ross, with a pref. by Raymond Aron. 208 p. Boston, Beacon Press. 1962
Sociologie de l'Algérie, Paris, 1958

Algeria 1960: The Disenchantment of the World; The Sense of Honour; The Kabyle House or the World Reversed: Essays / by Pierre Bourdieu; translated by Richard Nice. Cambridge (Eng.); New York: Cambridge University Press, 1979
Algerie 60

Bourdieu: Critical Perspectives. Edited by Craig Calhoun, Edward LiPuma, and Moishe Postone. A product of a conference held at the Center for Psychosocial Studies in Chicago, March 31 – April 2, 1989. 288 p.; Chicago: University of Chicago Press, 1993.

The Craft of Sociology: Epistemological Preliminaries / Pierre Bourdieu, Jean-Claude Chamboredon, Jean-Claude Passeron; edited by Beate Krais; translated by Richard Nice. 271 pp. Berlin; New York: Walter de Gruyter, 1991
Le métier du sociologue, second French edition, Paris, Mouton [1973] 357 p.

Distinction: A Social Critique of the Judgment of Taste / Pierre Bourdieu; translated by Richard Nice. Cambridge, 613 pp., Mass.: Harvard University Press, 1984
La distinction: critique sociale du jugement. 670 pp., Paris: Éditions de Minuit, 1979.

La domination masculine. 142 pp. Paris]: Seuil, 1998

Les étudiants et leurs etudes / Pierre Bourdieu, Jean-Claude Passeron in collaboration with Michel Eliard. 149 pp. Paris: Mouton, 1964

The Field of Cultural Production: Essays on Art and Literature. Edited and introduced by Randal Johnson. 322 pp., New York: Columbia University Press, 1993

Free Exchange / Pierre Bourdieu and Hans Haacke. 144 pp. Stanford, Calif.: Stanford University Press, 1995

Libre-échange 147 p. Paris: Seuil: Presses du réel, c1994

Homo Academicus. Translated by Peter Collier. Stanford, Calif.: Stanford University Press, 1988.
Homo academicus. 302 pp. Paris: Editions de Minuit, c1984

In Other Words: Essays Towards a Reflexive Sociology. "Choses dites", with two additional essays. Translated by Matthew Adamson. 223 pp., Cambridge: Polity Press, 1990; Stanford, CA: Stanford University Press, 1990 Choses dites, 229 pp., Paris: Les Éditions de Minuit, 1987

The Inheritors: French Students and Their Relation to Culture / Pierre Bourdieu and Jean-Claude Passeron; translated by Richard Nice. Chicago: University of Chicago Press, 1979
Les heritiers, les etudiants et la culture.

An Invitation to Reflexive Sociology. Bourdieu, Pierre and Loïc Wacquant xvi, 332 p. Chicago: The University of Chicago Press, 1992
Réponses: pour une anthropologie réflexive / Pierre Bourdieu, avec Loïc J. D. Wacquant. 267 p. Paris: Seuil, 1992

Language and symbolic power / Pierre Bourdieu; edited and introduced by John B. Thompson; translated by Gino Raymond and Matthew Adamson. 302 p. Cambridge, Mass.: Harvard University Press, 1991

Ce que parler veut dire: l'économie des échanges linguistiques, 243 p. , Paris: Fayard, c1982

Leçon inaugurale: Friday, April 23, 1982. 36 p., [Paris]: Collège de France, 1982
Leçon sur la leçon / Pierre Bourdieu. 55 p. Paris: Editions de Minuit, c1982

The Logic of Practice / Pierre Bourdieu; translated by Richard Nice. 330 p. Stanford, Calif.: Stanford University Press, 1990
Le sens pratique. 475 p. Paris: Éditions de Minuit, c1980

The Love of Art: European Art Museums and Their Public / Pierre Bourdieu and Alain Darbel with Dominique Schnapper; translated by Caroline Beattie and Nick Merriman Stanford, Calif.: Stanford University Press, 1990.
L'Amour de l'art. les musées d'art européens et leur public. Paris, les Éditions de Minuit, 1969

On Television / Pierre Bourdieu; translated from the French by Priscilla Parkhurst Ferguson. New York: New Press: Distributed by W.W. Norton, c1998
Sur la television.

Outline of A Theory of Practice / with revisions. Translated by Richard Nice. Cambridge; New York: Cambridge University Press, 1977 (reprinted 1989)
Esquisse d'une théorie de la pratique. Précédé de trois etudes d'ethnologie kabyle. 269 pp., Genève [Paris] Droz, 1972

Pascalian Meditations. Translated by Richard Nice 256 p., Stanford, Calif.: Stanford University Press, 2000
Méditations pascaliennes. 316 p. Paris: Seuil, 1997

Photography: A Middle-brow Art / Pierre Bourdieu, with Luc Boltanski ... (et al.); translated by Shaun Whiteside Stanford, Calif.: Stanford University Press, 1990
Photographie: Art Moyen, essai sur les usages sociaux de la photographie.

The Political Ontology of Martin Heidegger. Translated by Peter Collier. 138 p. Stanford, Calif.: Stanford University Press, 1991
L'ontologie politique de Martin Heidegger 122 p. Paris: Éditions de Minuit, c1988

Practical Reason: On the Theory of Action. 153 p. Stanford, Calif.: Stanford University Press, 1998
Raisons pratiques: sur la théorie de l'action. 251 p. Paris: Seuil, 1994

Reproduction in Education, Society and Culture / Pierre Bourdieu and Jean-Claude Passeron; Rev. ed. / preface to the 1990 edition by Pierre Bourdieu. Translated by Richard Nice; with a foreword by Tom Bottomore. 254 p. London: Sage, 1990
La reproduction; éléments pour une théorie du système d'enseignement.

Pierre Bourdieu et Jean-Claude Passeron

The Rules of Art: Genesis and Structure of the Literary Field. Translated by Susan Emanuel. 408 p. Stanford, Calif.: Stanford University Press, 1996
Les règles de l'art: genèse et structure du champ littéraire. 480 p. Paris]: Seuil, c1992

Social Theory for a Changing Society / edited by Pierre Bourdieu and James S. Coleman Boulder: Westview Press; New York: Russell Sage Foundation, 1991

Sociology in Question. Translated by Richard Nice 184 p. London: Sage, 1993
Questions de sociologie. 277 p., Paris: Minuit, 1980

The State Nobility: Elite Schools in the Field of Power; translated by Lauretta C. Clough. 475 p. Stanford, CA: Stanford University Press, 1996
La Noblesse d'état: grandes écoles et esprit de corps. 568 p., Paris: Éditions de minuit, 1989

The Weight of the World: Social Suffering in Contemporary Society / Pierre Bourdieu et al.; translated by Pricilla Parkhurst Ferguson [et al.]. 646 p., Stanford, Calif.: Stanford University Press, 1999
La Misère du monde.

Also from Algora Publishing:

CLAUDIU A. SECARA
THE NEW COMMONWEALTH
From Bureaucratic Corporatism to Socialist Capitalism

The notion of an elite-driven worldwide perestroika has gained some credibility lately. The book examines in a historical perspective the most intriguing dialectic in the Soviet Union's "collapse" — from socialism to capitalism and back to socialist capitalism — and speculates on the global implications.

IGNACIO RAMONET
THE GEOPOLITICS OF CHAOS

The author, Director of *Le Monde Diplomatique,* presents an original, discriminating and lucid political matrix for understanding what he calls the "current disorder of the world" in terms of Internationalization, Cyberculture and Political Chaos.

TZVETAN TODOROV
A PASSION FOR DEMOCRACY –
Benjamin Constant

The French Revolution rang the death knell not only for a form of society, but also for a way of feeling and of living; and it is still not clear as yet what did we gain from the changes.

MICHEL PINÇON & MONIQUE PINÇON-CHARLOT
GRAND FORTUNES –
Dynasties of Wealth in France

Going back for generations, the fortunes of great families consist of far more than money—they are also symbols of culture and social interaction. In a nation known for democracy and meritocracy, piercing the secrets of the grand fortunes verges on a crime of lèse-majesté . . . *Grand Fortunes* succeeds at that.

CLAUDIU A. SECARA
TIME & EGO –
Judeo-Christian Egotheism and the Anglo-Saxon Industrial Revolution

The first question of abstract reflection that arouses controversy is the problem of Becoming. Being persists, beings constantly change; they are born and they pass away. How can Being change and yet be eternal? The quest for the logical and experimental answer has just taken off.

JEAN-MARIE ABGRALL
SOUL SNATCHERS: THE MECHANICS OF CULTS

Jean-Marie Abgrall, psychiatrist, criminologist, expert witness to the French Court of Appeals, and member of the Inter-Ministry Committee on Cults, is one of the experts most frequently consulted by the European judicial and legislative processes. The fruit of fifteen years of research, his book delivers the first methodical analysis of the sectarian phenomenon, decoding the mental manipulation on behalf of mystified observers as well as victims.

JEAN-CLAUDE GUILLEBAUD
THE TYRANNY OF PLEASURE

Guillebaud, a Sixties' radical, re-thinks liberation, taking a hard look at the question of sexual morals -- that is, the place of the forbidden -- in a modern society. For almost a whole generation, we have lived in the illusion that this question had ceased to exist. Today the illusion is faded, but a strange and tumultuous distress replaces it. No longer knowing very clearly where we stand, our societies painfully seek answers between unacceptable alternatives: bold-faced permissiveness or nostalgic moralism.

SOPHIE COIGNARD AND MARIE-THÉRÈSE GUICHARD
FRENCH CONNECTIONS –
The Secret History of Networks of Influence

They were born in the same region, went to the same schools, fought the same fights and made the same mistakes in youth. They share the same morals, the same fantasies of success and the same taste for money. They act behind the scenes to help each other, boosting careers, monopolizing business and information, making money, conspiring and, why not, becoming Presidents!

VLADIMIR PLOUGIN
RUSSIAN INTELLIGENCE SERVICES. Vol. I. Early Years

Mysterious episodes from Russia's past – alliances and betrayals, espionage and military feats – are unearthed and examined in this study, which is drawn from ancient chronicles and preserved documents from Russia, Greece, Byzantium and the Vatican Library. Scholarly analysis and narrative flair combine to give both the facts and the flavor of the battle scenes and the espionage milieu, including the establishment of secret services in Kievan rus, the heroes and the techniques of intelligence and counter-intelligence in the 10th-12th centuries, and the times of Vladimir.

JEAN-JACQUES ROSA
EURO ERROR

The European Superstate makes Jean-Jacques Rosa mad, for two reasons. First, actions taken to relieve unemployment have created inflation, but have not reduced unemployment. His second argument is even more intriguing: the 21st century will see the fragmentation of the U. S., not the unification of Europe.

ANDRÉ GAURON
EUROPEAN MISUNDERSTANDING

Few of the books decrying the European Monetary Union raise the level of the discussion to a higher plane. *European Misunderstanding* is one of these. Gauron gets it right, observing that the real problem facing Europe is its political future, not its economic future.

Dominique Fernandez
Photographer: Ferrante Ferranti
ROMANIAN RHAPSODY — An Overlooked Corner of Europe

"Romania doesn't get very good press." And so, renowned French travel writer Dominique Fernandez and top photographer Ferrante Ferranti head out to form their own images. In four long journeys over a 6-year span, they uncover a tantalizing blend of German efficiency and Latin nonchalance, French literature and Gypsy music, Western rationalism and Oriental mysteries. Fernandez reveals the rich Romanian essence. Attentive and precise, he digs beneath the somber heritage of communism to reach the deep roots of a European country that is so little-known.

Philippe Trétiack
ARE YOU AGITÉ? Treatise on Everyday Agitation

"A book filled with the exuberance of a new millennium, full of humor and relevance. Philippe Trétiack, a leading reporter for *Elle*, goes around the world and back, taking an interest in the futile as well as the essential. His flair for words, his undeniable culture, help us to catch on the fly what we really are: characters subject to the ballistic impulse of desires, fads and a click of the remote. His book invites us to take a healthy break from the breathless agitation in general." —*Aujourd'hui le Parisien*

"The 'Agité,' that human species that lives in international airports, jumps into taxis while dialing the cell phone, eats while clearing the table, reads the paper while watching TV and works during vacation – has just been given a new title." — *Le Monde des Livres*

Paul Lombard
VICE & VIRTUE — Men of History, Great Crooks for the Greater Good

Personal passion has often guided powerful people more than the public interest. With what result? From the courtiers of Versailles to the back halls of Mitterand's government, from Danton — revealed to have been a paid agent for England — to the shady bankers of Mitterand's era, from the buddies of Mazarin to the builders of the Panama Canal, Paul Lombard unearths the secrets of the corridors of power. He reveals the vanity and the corruption, but also the grandeur and panache that characterize the great. This cavalcade over many centuries can be read as a subversive tract on how to lead.

Richard Labévière
DOLLARS FOR TERROR — The U.S. and Islam

"In this riveting, often shocking analysis, the U.S. is an accessory in the rise of Islam, because it manipulates and aids radical Moslem groups in its shortsighted pursuit of its economic interests, especially the energy resources of the Middle East and the oil- and mineral-rich former Soviet republics of Central Asia. Labévière shows how radical Islamic fundamentalism spreads its influence on two levels, above board, through investment firms, banks and shell companies, and clandestinely, though a network of drug dealing, weapons smuggling and money laundering. This important book sounds a wake-up call to U.S. policy-makers." — *Publishers Weekly*

JEANNINE VERDÈS-LEROUX

DECONSTRUCTING PIERRE BOURDIEU

Against Sociological Terrorism From the Left

Sociologist Pierre Bourdieu went from widely-criticized to widely-acclaimed, without adjusting his hastily constructed theories. Turning the guns of critical analysis on his own critics, he was happier jousting in the ring of (often quite undemocratic) political debate than reflecting and expanding upon his own propositions. Verdès-Leroux has spent 20 years researching the policy impact of intellectuals who play at the fringes of politics. She suggests that Bourdieu arrogated for himself the role of "total intellectual" and proved that a good offense is the best defense. A pessimistic Leninist bolstered by a ponderous scientific construct, Bourdieu stands out as the ultimate doctrinaire more concerned with self-promotion than with democratic intellectual engagements.

HENRI TROYAT

TERRIBLE TZARINAS

Who should succeed Peter the Great? Upon the death of this visionary and despotic reformer, the great families plotted to come up with a successor who would surpass everyone else — or at least, offend none. But there were only women — Catherine I, Anna Ivanovna, Anna Leopoldovna, Elizabeth I. These autocrats imposed their violent and dissolute natures upon the empire, along with their loves, their feuds, their cruelties. Born in 1911 in Moscow, Troyat is a member of the Académie française, recipient of Prix Goncourt.

JEAN-MARIE ABGRALL

HEALERS OR STEALERS — Medical Charlatans in the New Age

Jean-Marie Abgrall is Europe's foremost expert on cults and forensic medicine. He asks, are fear of illness and death the only reasons why people trust their fates to the wizards of the pseudo-revolutionary and the practitioners of pseudo-magic? We live in a bazaar of the bizarre, where everyday denial of rationality has turned many patients into ecstatic fools. While not all systems of nontraditional medicine are linked to cults, this is one of the surest avenues of recruitment, and the crisis of the modern world may be leading to a new mystique of medicine where patients check their powers of judgment at the door.

DR. DEBORAH SCHURMAN-KAUFLIN

THE NEW PREDATOR: WOMEN WHO KILL — Profiles of Female Serial Killers

This is the *first book ever* based on face-to-face interviews with women serial killers.